Our Life's
Journey

GOD WAS ALWAYS THERE

DICK & JERI INGRAM

WESTBOW
PRESS®
A DIVISION OF THOMAS NELSON
& ZONDERVAN

WestBow Press books may be ordered through
booksellers or by contacting:

WestBow Press
A Division of Thomas Nelson & Zondervan
1663 Liberty Drive
Bloomington, IN 47403
www.westbowpress.com
844-714-3454

ISBN: 978-1-6642-6522-6 (sc)
ISBN: 978-1-6642-6521-9 (e)

Library of Congress Control Number: 2022907864

Print information available on the last page.

WestBow Press rev. date: 05/13/2022

Contents

Dedication

To all husbands, wives, parents, pastors, hard-working people everywhere who wonder if God really sees and cares about what you're going through, this book is for you!

God created you and He wants to help you. Let this book be an encouragement to you that God will intervene in your lives in ways both big and small, ways you never dreamed possible. He loves you and He will never leave you alone.

Special Thanks

OUR FAMILY —We truly have the most wonderful family for which a person could ever ask. We want to say THANK YOU to our beautiful daughters, Kimberly and Kristina, who have stood with us and served with us and ministered to us on a daily basis in more ways than we could ever count. We want to thank our incredible sons-in-law, Tim and Tom, who have been reliable strong arms to lean on. And we want to say a very special thank you to our adorable grandsugars, Cody and his beautiful wife Sierra, Kaylee, Christopher, Corey and Chloe. They have been our angels constantly spreading light, love and joy into our lives. There simply are not enough ways to say how much we love you.

MY SISTER, MAGGIE — I, Jeri, would like to take this opportunity to thank my sister, Maggie, for all her help with this book. Her major in college was English with a Writing Option, and I appreciate the hours she spent using her skills to help with the editing. Along with that, she also used her technological expertise to help me with compiling the project. I will always be grateful for the time and care she so generously gave.

PASTORS LOU & KRIS ZINNANTI — We first met Pastors Lou and Kris when they were a young, newlywed couple, and we were all witnessing for the Lord on the streets of the inner city of Philadelphia. The faithfulness and fervency they demonstrated to the work of God, even as such a young couple, was a joy to watch. Little did we know that, many years later, as we reached our retirement, the Lord would bring this same dynamic young couple to take our place as Sr. Pastors of this wonderful church that we had loved and pastored for twenty-six years. Now we watch with grateful hearts as they serve with the same faithfulness and fervency we saw on the inner city streets of Philadelphia so many years ago, and we cannot be more grateful for their love and dedication. The plans of God are so amazing!

Foreword

By Joe Fitzgerald, Boston Herald

What you are holding in your hands right now is a magnificent piece of work authored by two dear friends of mine, Dick & Jeri Ingram, who set out to take us on a guided tour of God's sovereignty and goodness through the fifty-six years of their marriage and the lifetime they have spent together in ministry.

Their idea was to create a handy journal, a series of anecdotes and observations designed to bolster any reader's walk with the Lord through the power of their own examples, which is just another way of saying 'personal testimonies'. We don't hear as much about them as we once did, do we? Yet, they can still have a mighty impact on anyone who will take the time to 'taste and see', as you are now.

Like the Apostle Paul, Dick and Jeri were not hoping to impress anyone with the eloquence of their words, though their words are indeed eloquent; instead, they simply wanted to lift up the name of Jesus by sharing how He has blessed their endeavors and directed their paths as He promised He would.

This is essentially a collection of parables, which long ago we were taught were 'earthly stories with heavenly meanings,' remember? Chances are, you are going to find your own stories somewhere in these pages so enjoy and let it bless you!

Introduction

We originally wrote this book to be used as a daily devotional, but it has evolved into something much more than that. Rather, it has become a book of personal stories filled with Biblical truths we have learned over fifty six years of marriage.

I, Jeri, want to begin with the story of my parents who were buried one week apart. My dad was buried one Saturday, and the very next Saturday we buried my mom. Some might think that was a terrible tragedy, but our family viewed it as something beautiful that honored the close relationship they had always shared for sixty-two years of marriage. They never wanted to be apart.

When my husband was sharing at my mother's funeral about the closeness my parents had enjoyed, he made a statement I have never forgotten. He said, "Tinky and Gerald had a rendezvous in Heaven and now they are dancing on streets of gold."

They left a wonderful legacy for married couples in a time when the institution of marriage is under such onslaught. As I thought about that, and looked back over our own life and the journey we shared, it seemed like a dance to me – flowing together, growing together, supporting each other, laughing and crying together, enjoying each other, which is what I think God had in mind when He created marriage.

This book is our way of looking back over our life together and remembering all the times that God supernaturally stepped in and intervened in amazing ways – both big and small – to help us. We were never intended to walk through life alone – without the help of God. We need Him! And the wonderful thing is, He is always right there, more than ready to help us. All we have to do is ask!

Our Words Have Power

By Dick Ingram

A gentle answer turns away wrath, but a harsh
word stirs up anger. Proverbs 15:1 (NIV)

As a pastor with two young daughters, it was vitally
important to my wife and me that we live our Christian
lives as transparently as we possibly could. We continually
emphasized to them the importance of committing God's
Word to memory, and we tried to remind ourselves that our
actions speak much louder than our words.

One morning my girls, Kimberly and Kristina, were with
me as I stopped by the post office to pick up the mail. As
we were pulling into the post office parking lot, I didn't
see a young man on his motorcycle, and I almost ran over
him. The near accident frightened him, and he angrily
demonstrated his displeasure through a well-known hand
gesture as he ran up to my car trembling with anger. As
I rolled down my window, he began to yell all kind of
obscenities at me. I apologized profusely for scaring him so
badly and asked if he would please refrain from using such
language in front of my young daughters who were in the
car with me. I asked if he would please forgive me for my
careless actions. My kindness baffled him so that he couldn't
say a word. He just stared and then walked away from the

car, once again waving his hand gesture as he got onto his motorcycle and left.

When we drove off, it was very quiet in the car, and my girls appeared a bit stunned from it all, so I pulled to the side of the road to see if I could encourage them. I was deeply saddened at the course of events. It was then that my oldest daughter, Kimberly, nine years old at the time, soberly said to me, "Dad, the scriptures are true. You gave a kind answer, and it turned away his wrath." I was so taken back by her words and so proud of her that I could not hold back my tears. I had lived out the Christian example before my girls, and they recognized the scripture I was obeying. Our children are watching us while we are molding their lives daily by our own examples. It's important that we do it right!

Prayer

Lord, help me to live my life today in a way that demonstrates Jesus to my children. Let them see the wisdom, power and love of Jesus through my actions all day. Amen

An Ambassador of Heaven

By Dick Ingram

Therefore, as God's chosen people, holy
and dearly loved, clothe yourselves with
compassion, kindness, humility, gentleness
and patience. Colossians 3:12 (NIV)

I was a young Houston police officer when my wife and I found salvation through Christ Jesus. The immediate changes that took place in our lives and our lifestyle were huge! We began to view life and its challenges from a Christ-like perspective. As 2 Corinthians 5:17 (KJV) says, "old things are passed away, behold, all things are become new."

As a police officer, I constantly dealt with the dark side of life, and before I gave my heart to Christ, I looked at life and people from a cynical viewpoint. Typically, the last thing most officers want to hear over their car radio is the order to "pick up the winos at the blood bank and book them." We would circle the block over and over, hoping the smelly winos would leave before we arrived. Once you put them in your police car, the odor remained in the car for the rest of the shift, and you could not get it out.

On my first day at work after becoming a Christian, my partner was shocked by my change in attitude—I was even shocked myself! I no longer saw the winos as objects of scorn but instead saw them as precious souls who were made in the image of God. I began to treat them differently. When the dispatcher sent me to the blood bank, they did not seem like the scum of the earth anymore but rather souls desperately needing a Savior. I began to understand that I was sent there by the city of Houston as the arresting officer, but I was sent by God as an ambassador of heaven.

One afternoon, the streets on skid row were unusually full of drunks, so our sergeant ordered a paddy wagon. As we were loading the men onto the wagon, I noticed one man was missing a leg, and I felt great compassion for him. With my fellow officers looking at me with great disdain, I put my arm around him and told him to wait till the others were loaded so he wouldn't trip and fall. Then I gently lifted him up into the paddy wagon. As we were shutting the doors, the crippled man looked at me with tears in his eyes and said, "Thanks, Officer. There is sure something different about you." As I walked away, a tear rolled down my cheek. I, too, had once been lost, but now I was found. Bill and Gloria Gaither said it best in their song "Thanks to Calvary":

> Today I went back to the place where we used to live,
> My little boy ran and hid behind the door.
> I said, son, never fear, you've got a new daddy,
> Thanks to Calvary, we don't live here anymore.

If you have received Jesus Christ as your Savior, don't hesitate to allow kindness, gentleness, and compassion to flow from your life. That is what makes a distinctive difference in you from the rest of the world. That is what will draw people to want to know you and will open doors for you to share about this wonderful Savior.

Prayer
Father, please help me today to show the love of Christ to all with whom I come in contact. Help me to keep my eyes open and my heart softened toward hurting humanity, and to continually remember that "there but for the grace of Grace of God go I." Amen.

Giving Honor Is A Lifetime Event

By Dick Ingram

Children, obey your parents in the Lord,
for this is right. Honor your father and
mother, which is the first commandment
with promise, so that it may be well with
you, and you may live long on the earth.
Ephesians 6:1–3 (NIV)

Children honoring and obeying their parents is important to the Lord. God wants parents to teach this important lesson to their children as they are growing up. When I was nine years old, my father found Christ at the bedside of my dying brother, Freddie, who was just thirteen. After that, my dad never missed a church service and neither did I nor my younger brother, Gary. From that moment on, we couldn't have been raised in a more wonderful, loving Christian home. Honoring my father and mother wasn't a difficult thing for me even as such a young boy. There was one time, though, when I was in the eighth grade that I dishonored my parents, and it taught me a lesson that is still vivid in my mind today, many years later.

As a young teenager, I was in a challenging stage of life, and my parents were concerned about my lack of interest in my schoolwork. My dad had warned me not to bring home any D's on my report card, or it would mean a trip to the proverbial woodshed. Sure enough, as my friend Alf and I were perusing our next report cards, there were two ugly D's that stood out like an eighteen-wheeler truck bearing down on me! Together we concluded that my only option was to run away from home, and my trusty friend Alf agreed to go with me. By nightfall we had covered sixteen miles on foot, dodging truant officers as though we were fleeing felons. It was dark and cold and scary as we huddled behind a 7-11 store. I finally decided to call my parents to come and get us. They were just about out of their minds with worry.

As I saw my dad pull up in that ugly old Nash, I trembled at what I might encounter. Alf and I climbed in the back seat for a very quiet, long ride home. My dad never said a word, but there were tears pouring down his cheeks the entire time that said it all. The pain those tears inflicted on my heart did more for me than any trip to the woodshed could have done. Even today, many years later, I fight back tears as I remember his face. That life lesson of honoring my father and mother didn't just affect me as an eighth grader; I am still walking in that honor for them today!

I encourage you today, teach your children this vital life lesson. If they learn at a young age to value and respect the guidance and instruction of their parents, it could save them a lot of trouble as they go through the turbulent teenage years.

PRAYER

Showing honor to whom honor is due is a vital part of the culture of the kingdom of heaven. Help my children to learn this life lesson, and help me to set the right example before them by honoring you and showing honor to those who have authority over my life. Amen.

A Truthful Word, Though Painful, Produces Hope

By Dick Ingram

> He who rebukes a man shall afterward find
> more favor than he who flatters with his
> tongue. Proverbs 28:23 (NLT)

Many years ago, I entered Southwestern Assemblies of God University as a new Christian and student with hopes and dreams of studying to become a minister of the gospel. What a blessing those college years proved to be under the guidance of gifted teachers, skilled by years of working the mission field, pastoring churches, and counseling hurting people; all had been through the school of hard knocks. Yes, they held master's degrees and doctorates, but they were even more skilled in "knee-ology," the art of lying prostrate in the presence of God. Some had battled face-to-face deep darkness in jungles on foreign soil. I cherished the days I sat in their classrooms, visited with them in their school offices or at the coffee shop – just soaking up their knowledge!

As I was sitting in chapel one day, a message in tongues was given. (ICor.12:10 KJV). I knew I had the interpretation, but I was a new Christian, and I was afraid to give it, so I kept silent. As the day went on, I felt increasingly distressed that I had failed God. By the end of that day, I had fallen drastically over the cliff of depression. The next day I sat through all my classes feeling totally condemned.

I knew I needed help, so finally I went to Rev. Hugh Jeter's office who was the Missions Director and a veteran missionary to Cuba. Bro. Jeter had given me excellent council in the past, so I felt sure he could help me again. As I unburdened my heart to him, I saw the look in his eyes change from compassion to a look of pain. When I had finished reciting my pity-party confession, Bro. Jeter pushed back from his desk and proceeded to read me the riot act.

He sternly said, "Do you think you are the only one who has ever failed God or made a mistake? Does one failure mean you are all washed up in the ministry and it's time to go home? If this failure has so defeated you, what will the next one do? Is God so upset with you He doesn't ever want to see your face again? Dick Ingram, get a grip! Stop your pity party! Shake yourself and ask God to forgive you and strengthen you to be more obedient to His commands! You are a baby Christian just learning who God really is. He is a loving, nurturing Father who is anxious to see us mature from drinking milk to eating meat. Do not waste another minute in this melancholy valley you are in. Get out of my office, put a happy smile on your face and go learn about the grace of God!"

Wow! Talk about being blown away! I felt like my hair was blowing back and my eyes squinting at the force of his words. At first, I thought it was harsh, but then I heard a still, small voice inside me say, "No, it wasn't"!

I left the building in a daze, but by the time I got outside a slight smile broke across my face. As I slowly digested his council, I began to feel better and better. By that evening I felt I had a new lease on life. Later, I even came to understand that his words to me were like "apples of gold in baskets of silver". (Proverbs 25:11 KJV)

Now it is almost half a century later, and I am retired from active ministry, but my advice to young ministers just beginning their journey is the same as it has always been. Find yourself a godly mentor or mentors that you trust, and glean all you can from them. Thank God for your youth, energy and vitality. The church of Jesus Christ desperately needs you. But never discount or minimize the value of the wisdom and experience of the elders who have gone before you. Together, we are the BODY OF CHRIST in action!!!

PRAYER – Lord, give me wise mentors to speak into my life. Give me a humble spirit to receive whatever instruction, correction or encouragement you would speak to me through their lives. Thank you for loving me enough to help me continue growing. AMEN

My Father's Legacy

By Dick Ingram

A good man leaveth an inheritance to his
children's children. Proverbs 13:22 (KJV)

The older I get the more I realize how important it is to be
aware of the kind of legacy we will leave behind. The more
we think about what our legacy will be, the more motivated
we will be to live our lives in a godly way. My dad was a
supreme example in this area. He changed from being a
wild, partying, drinking young man in his early years to
becoming one of the most vibrant, steadfast, Christ-like
men I ever knew. He definitely left a powerful inheritance
and legacy to his children and his grandchildren.

Some years ago, when my dad was in his early 70's, we
were driving together through the town in which he had
grown up. He had been unusually quiet and then suddenly
he began to weep. I was startled and I quickly blurted out,
"Dad, what's wrong? Are you alright?"

When he finally regained his composure, he solemnly said,
"As we were driving down these old familiar streets I began
to think about the years when I lived as a wild young man
before the love of Christ transformed my life. I can't help
but wonder how many children I fathered during those years

that were left to grow up without a dad." His tears began to flow again.

When my dad became a born-again believer, there was a radical change in his life. He is in heaven now, but he is definitely my hero, for once he found Christ he lived the most exemplary life I've ever known and touched more lives than I could count.

He was a simple man, a welder by trade, whose life was devoted to others. He didn't teach a Sunday School class, and he sure couldn't sing, but he loved people with a deep and genuine love. Every week he did things like mowing the yards of every widow in our church. He regularly drove cancer patients to the cancer center in downtown Houston for their treatments. One time his CPA pulled him aside and said, "Red, you are giving too much money to God. It's absolutely astounding how much money you give." My dad just laughed and said, "You can't outgive God!"

My dad owned some boat storages he built for a retirement income, and I'll never forget the year they all burned down. He received a phone call in the middle of the night. He jumped in his car, still in his bathrobe, and raced down there, fearlessly running from stall to stall through flames and smoke unlocking each door to help the firemen gain quick access.

After the fire was out, the storages were pretty much destroyed and we were devastated. I looked at my dad and asked what he was going to do. With a big grin on his face, he looked at me and said, "Well, lad-y-o (his favorite nickname for me), we're gonna rebuild!" Immediately, he started tearing down boards & sweeping off the foundation to get it ready. The rebuilding started soon after that, and in a short time we had brand-new boat storages!

He was one of those quiet heroes, but when he died, his funeral was so large it had to be held in the largest church in town. From the family car I looked back at the streams of cars following us and it seemed miles long. As we pulled into the cemetery, six motorcycle police officers stood at attention in honor of my dad. I couldn't help but think, "Thanks, Dad, for the incredible heritage you left us."

This is God's desire for you – to live your life in such a devoted way that the next generation can look at you and be inspired to say, "I want to live my life in that way!"

PRAYER - My prayer today is for dads everywhere, that we become the kind of men God wants us to be, the kind of men who can leave behind a legacy and an inheritance that will enrich the lives of our families & friends. May God help us each to be that kind of man! AMEN

Today's Idle Word ...
Tomorrow's Judgment

By Dick Ingram

> But I say unto you, that every idle word that men
> shall speak, they shall give account thereof in
> the Day of Judgment. Matthew 12:36 (KJV)

How many times have we read a certain scripture over and over again without a real connection, then on another day that same scripture leaps off the page at you? A short while ago I was reading the scripture about speaking idle words and it seemed to shout at me ... pay attention!!! The Disciples' Literal New Testament reads, "And I say to you that every useless word which people will speak, they will render an account for it on the day of judgment. For by your words you will be declared righteous, and by your words you will be condemned." How many times have I spoken a word to someone and regretted it immediately. I went home wishing I could take back those idle useless, senseless words. You have heard the saying, "sticks and stones may break my bones, but words will never hurt me". Not true! Words can injure and destroy lives.

When I was still serving as a Houston police officer, one day I pulled over a car in downtown Houston and the driver turned out to be a Houston emergency hospital doctor. He was out showing his family the sights, and when I walked up to the car, he looked very agitated with me. When I told him he had made a dangerous, illegal turn from a third lane, he tore into me, saying, "You better hope I never get you in my emergency room"! I was stunned, and immediately issued him a hefty ticket. As he drove off, mumbling under his breath, I went straight to my police three-wheeler motorcycle, grabbed a pen, and wrote down on the backside of my copy of the ticket all the choice words he had said to me.

Later, as I suspected, he showed up in court to dispute the so-called 'unfair ticket'. After the doctor told the judge why he felt he was innocent, the judge asked me if the doctor had said anything to me, so I turned over the ticket and read the choice words he had spoken. I could see the judge's face turning red! When I finished speaking, the judge threw the book at him and lectured him on how to treat "Houston's finest"! The recorded words of the doctor cost him dearly when he stood before the judge.

One day we will all stand before our Heavenly Judge as He reads from the Book of Life. My prayer is we will hear Him say, 'well done, thou good and faithful servant!'

PRAYER – Lord, set a watch over my lips today. Let my words be only words of kindness, encouragement and building up others. If I start to say idle words, give me a nudge to keep me on the right path. AMEN

Visions & Dreams

By Dick Ingram

Whether I was in my body or out of my body,
I don't know – only God knows. Yes, only
God knows whether I was in my body or
outside my body. But I do know that I was
caught up to paradise and heard things so
astounding that they cannot be expressed in
words, things no human is allowed to tell. 2
Corinthians 12:2-4 (NLT)

Not long after I became a born-again Christian I had a most unusual encounter with the Lord. One day, on my way to roll call as a Houston police officer, I decided to stop by the hospital to visit a wonderful Christian brother who was near death. When I walked into his room I saw his family there, and as I approached his bedside, I noticed an incredibly beautiful aura around him, and I felt the presence of the Lord so powerfully, I felt as though I had stepped through a veil into a most Holy Place.

His radiant smile said it all, and as he took my hand, we joined together in prayer, and it was unlike anything I've ever experienced before or since. As we prayed together, I felt enveloped in a cloud, and became unaware of the others in the room. The peace and joy were so tangible that I felt I could almost physically touch it!

As we prayed, I began to hear the voices of his family off in the distance. They had stepped closer to the bed and were urgently saying, "It's ok! Everything is ok!" My friend and I had not realized how loud we were praying and worshipping God, and it seemed to give his family concern.

As I left the room, my Christian friend with whom I had been praying gave me a look that seemed to say, "I'll see you on the other side!" A few days later he crossed the bar.

I stepped into the hallway of the hospital and could see the nurses busy at the nursing station, yet I noticed a cloud that separated us and made them seem far away. Once I was outside of the hospital, I got onto my police three-wheeler motorcycle and headed for the police station sixteen miles away, and the cloud never left. I still felt enveloped!

As I drove, I began asking the Lord different questions that came into my mind, and the minute I asked the question, I immediately knew the answer. I kept asking questions as fast as I possibly could, and each time the answer instantly came. All of the answers to my questions that seemed so difficult to me were like kindergarten to God. I realized that in Heaven we will not need tongues and lips to talk. A mere thought is all that is necessary.

As I drew closer to the police station, I was so filled with God's presence and the joy of my new-found knowledge that I couldn't wait to share it with others, but just as I reached the station, the cloud began to fade. I cried, "Oh no, Lord! Please don't leave", but by the time I got into the room for roll call the cloud was gone, along with all the answers God had given me. I couldn't remember one word He had said.

I realized then that God had shared with me a glimpse into Heaven and what I had to look forward to. The glory and the awe and the pure joy of that experience has never left me.

PRAYER – Lord, fill me with your glory! Let me live my life so in tune with you and your wonderful presence that the sweet aura of the Holy Spirit will continually surround me, drawing people to hunger for a deeper walk with our Lord and Savior, Jesus Christ. AMEN

How To Stay In Perfect Peace

By Dick Ingram

> You will keep in perfect peace all who trust
> in you, all whose thoughts are fixed on you!
> Isaiah 26:3 (NLT)

I was 21 years old when I joined the Army. My first task was to go through Basic Training where the goal was to harden us and prepare us for the rigors of war.

One day they marched us to a plain, drab building, and as we entered the room they had us stand around the wall and handed us each a gas mask. As we put them on, the sergeant dropped a few small pellets into a pot in the middle of the room. Immediately the room began to fill with tear gas.

The sergeant then barked out these instructions, "When I say unmask, you will remove your gas masks and clearly call out your serial number. It's important that you stay clear headed, knowing that you are in a combat situation and you and your buddies' lives depend on your not being overcome with the pain and disorientation from the tear gas."

When I removed my mask, my nostrils were immediately on fire and breathing was very difficult. I just wanted to bolt for the door in panic, so I rapidly yelled out my serial number and raced for the door. A photographer took my picture as I exited. My eyes were squinted shut and my burning face was twisted in a strange looking contortion.

As a soldier I was commanded to keep my focus on winning the war and not be sidetracked by painful or stressful circumstances. As a Christian it is the same thing. Keep your eyes fixed on the Cross and the battle you are endeavoring to win. Don't allow pain, fear, worry, depression or circumstances to get your focus off the goal. Don't LET your heart be troubled. Keep your thoughts FIXED on the ONE who can help you and TRUST in Him, and you will have PERFECT PEACE. That is His promise!

PRAYER – Father, I pray today that you will help me to keep my thoughts fixed on you and your Word. I trust you to lead and guide my life and to help me in every situation. And I thank you for giving me perfect peace! AMEN

Let Your Light Shine!

By Dick Ingram

So don't hide your light! Let it shine brightly
before others, so that the commendable things
you do will shine as light upon them, and
then they will give their praise to your Father
in Heaven. Matthew 5:16 (TPT)

I was a Houston police officer when I found Christ, and at that moment in time my whole world changed drastically. I found myself filled with the desire to share my new faith, and I wasn't bashful about it.

My partner and I were in the Traffic Division and riding our police three-wheeler motorcycles together when I shared with him what had happened in my life. He wasn't a Christian so we had some intense and interesting conversations. My partner shared with me that several years earlier he was working in Austin, Texas, when a sniper went on a shooting spree killing innocent people on the Texas University campus. He saw his partner take a bullet to the head and die.

This tragedy haunted him, and he had become bitter, so when he learned I had become a Christian, he began harassing me daily about everything I did. He constantly hammered me with foul language, and the thought of going to work every day became something I dreaded. God helped me, however, to never lose my cool, for I did genuinely care about his soul.

Sometime later, I answered God's call to become a minister. I resigned from the police department, and on my last day I noticed my partner following me all the way from the third floor to the parking lot. When I got to the car I turned around to face him, not knowing if he was going to hug me or slug me!

To my surprise, he had tears in his eyes and handed me a gift. When I opened the box it was a beautiful sterling silver money clip. On the back was engraved the words, *To the Best Partner in the Houston Police Department.* Then he said, "All my life I have searched for something that was real. I know I have made your life miserable, but you have proved to me that the Lord is real and he is who he says he is!"

I never saw my partner again, but his face and words have followed me all these years. I showed him that God is real, but he showed me that it is not just what we say that counts; it's also the life we live.

PRAYER – Lord, I pray that you will remind me daily to let my light shine everywhere I go. Use me to make Christ real to a world that is in desperate need of a savior. AMEN

Angels Unaware

By Dick Ingram

Be not forgetful to entertain strangers:
for thereby some have entertained angels
unawares. Hebrews 13:2 (KJV)

Years ago, when I was a Houston police officer, an unusual event happened in my life. My partner and I had stopped at a Jack-in-the-Box to get something to eat. As we were sitting at a table, my eyes were drawn to a lady standing in line waiting to place her order. For some reason I felt there was something special about her. Her clothing was simple, but there was a radiance about her that was captivating.

I had only been a believer for about a year, but I realized that the presence of God was on her. When she got to the window she never placed an order. Instead she handed the worker something, smiled, and walked away. As she headed to the front door, I felt compelled to try and catch up to her. Within seconds I followed her out the front door, but she had disappeared from sight. The sidewalk was empty so I ran to the intersection and looked in all directions, but she wasn't there. In amazement, I stood there thinking, "That's impossible! I was only seconds behind her!"

I walked back inside and went over to the ordering window. There, laying on the counter, was a tract written about the Lord. That was the item she had handed to the worker. The Lord knows those who are ready to receive him, and it was obvious to me that God had sent an angel as a heavenly messenger to that worker who needed a savior!

From the beginning of time, angels have played an important part in the plans of God. Revelation 14 reveals an angel preaching the Gospel to all those who dwell on the earth at the end of time. In the meantime, He sends out angels everywhere to minister to His children, even when they are not aware that they are being ministered to by angels. That's why He instructed us to remember to show hospitality to strangers, because sometimes we are entertaining angels without even realizing it.

PRAYER – Father, I thank you for the Word of God that is a lamp unto our feet. Thank you for the guidance of the Holy Spirit, and thank you for sending angels to minister to us. Help me not to miss any opportunity to show hospitality to your angelic messengers. AMEN

The Prayer Of An Earthly Father

By Dick Ingram

> Now I know that you fear God, because you
> have not withheld from me your son, your
> only son. Genesis 22:12b (NIV)

In August of 1970, I entered Southwestern Assemblies of God University. Just three months later, our youngest daughter, Kristina, was born. Several months later she became very sick. We took her to the doctor and we gave her medicine, but she got worse and worse.

One night her fever was exceptionally high and she looked very bad, so we took her to bed with us. Just after getting into bed, a terrible Texas storm hit outside, and the thunder and lightning were violent. Her little eyes widened and searched my face for an assurance of safety. There was a terrible feeling of darkness and danger in the room, and I felt it was urgent that I touch the Lord on her behalf. I began to pray for her and tried to fight off the spirit of fear that was trying to consume me.

Suddenly, I heard the Lord, deep in my heart, say to me, "Will you release your child to me?" I was shaken to the core and found it hard to breath. Struggling, I said, "Is this a test, Lord? If I release her to you, will you take her to heaven?"

The tears began to flow as I struggled inside. The terrible storm going on outside was nothing compared to the storm going on inside of me. After some time of intense prayer, I finally yielded to the Lord's will for her life. It was hard to get the words out at first, but then I finally blurted out, "Lord, I give her totally and completely to you with all my heart and soul."

As soon as the words left my mouth, I couldn't believe the difference in me. It felt as though I was instantly cleansed from all doubt and fear. Over and over I sobbed, "I trust you, Lord!" The storm ended outside, and so did the storm inside me.

The next morning Kristina woke up healed and bright eyed. It was a miracle and I could not stop rejoicing over what God had done for our little girl. I felt the Lord was pleased that I had placed Him first in my life, even over my own child.

God promises us that if we place Him first in our lives, everything else will be taken care of. We serve a great and powerful and loving God!

PRAYER – Lord, I commit myself to making you first in my life. I pray for your grace to keep me on that path. Help me to never allow any idols to replace your rightful place as FIRST in my life. You created me and you saved me, and all that I have comes from you. Thank you for the privilege of serving you. AMEN

Who Should I Trust?

By Dick Ingram

The Lord is my strength and my defense.
Exodus 15:2 (NIV)

Years ago, when our oldest grandson, Cody, was about four years old, our family went into downtown Boston for a day of sightseeing. My wife, Jeri, and I thought it would be fun to take Cody for a horse and carriage ride, so the three of us nestled into the carriage with me on one seat, and Jeri and Cody on the opposite seat facing me.

As we got into the downtown area, suddenly the traffic became congested and the noise of a jackhammer breaking up concrete became deafening. The particular intersection we were driving through was under construction, and due to the noise, Cody immediately scooted over close to his grandmother, looked up at her with an earnest look and asked, "Does Papa have bravery?"

My wife immediately recognized his nervousness, so with great confidence, she replied, "Oh yes, Cody, Papa is very brave indeed!" Without a word, Cody hopped up and changed seats, sitting close beside me where he felt safe and protected. Cody loves his grandmother, but as a female he wasn't sure if she possessed the physical strength to give him adequate protection, so he decided to sit by me.

It is normal for a child to look to their parents or other adults in their lives for safety and protection, but as we grow up and mature we begin to realize that there are certain situations where human help is just not enough. Sometimes we find ourselves in situations so dangerous or difficult that only God Himself can help us. That is when God wants us to look to Him with confidence and realize He is our strength and our defense, and our trust should be in Him. Only the Lord can rescue us from the "jackhammers" of life!

PRAYER – Lord, I thank you for your loving care and protection for your children. I thank you that you care about every area of our lives – big or small! I trust you! AMEN

Conquering The Fear Of Flying

By Dick Ingram

> For though we walk in the flesh, we do
> not war after the flesh; for the weapons
> of our warfare are not carnal, but mighty
> through God to the pulling down of strong
> holds; casting down imaginations, and
> every high thing that exalts itself against the
> knowledge of God and bring into captivity
> every thought to the obedience of Christ.
> 2 Corinthians 10: 4-5 (KJV)

After graduating from high school, I joined the Army for a three-year tour of duty and was stationed with the 534th Military Police in Panama. One day the Army flew me from Panama to Houston on a very, very old military transport plane. We had mechanical trouble on takeoff and had to circle back with shark-infested waters only one hundred feet below us. The plane was wobbly and vibrating and some of the passengers began to panic, including myself.

We finally landed safely and were surrounded by fire engines, foam trucks and ambulances. My legs felt unsteady as I descended the stairs to the ground below, and that day became a defining moment for me. After that day, my flights could be described as white knuckle, and I entered into a phase of being terrified to fly. I was miserable.

After several years of living like that, I finally decided I had had enough! I had become a born-again Christian since that time, and was pastoring a church just outside of Houston, only a few miles from Hobby Airport. As a Christian, I knew the Bible teaches that "perfect love drives out fear" (I John 4:18 NIV), and I had been reading 2 Cor. 10:4-5 (KJV) that speaks about capturing rebellious thoughts and vain imaginations. I knew in my heart that God's Word was the answer to help me enjoy flying again.

Dallas was only 240 miles from Houston, so I decided to buy a round-trip ticket to Dallas. I brought my Bible along and loaded myself with a double barrel load of 2 Cor. 10:4-5 (KJV). During the short flight there and back, I kept reading over and over about casting down vain imaginations. I kept telling myself I would not go down in flames!

Once landing in Dallas, I immediately boarded my return flight and again quoted 2 Cor. 10:4-5 (KJV) over and over as I fought the fear of crashing.

It was expensive, but I continued doing this for a whole week. On the last day, as I boarded the plane for my return trip, I noticed I had no anxiety and the gnawing fear was gone. Since that time, I have joyfully flown to Germany and London and all over America – without a trace of fear!!! God's Word is truly powerful. I challenge you to allow the Word of God to become alive and powerful in your life!!

PRAYER – Lord, I pray that you would help me to overcome every fear in my life. I am standing on your Word, and I believe your power will set me free. Thank you for helping me. AMEN

Cherish Your Family

By Jeri Ingram

Be ye doers of the Word and not hearers only,
deceiving your own selves. James 1:22 (KJV)

FAMILY! What a beautiful word! I remember when it was the most prized and cherished institution in our country; yet, sadly, families today have become fragmented, weakened, and often destroyed. I was a high school student when a couple we had known for many years got a divorce. It was the first time I had ever personally known someone who was divorcing. They were a lovely middle aged couple with two fine teenage boys. They had been married for many years and were highly thought of in the community and respected in the large Methodist church we attended. I was stunned! It just did not make sense to me, and I was saddened for days after hearing the news.

As I look back at that time when divorce was almost unheard of and see how divorce today has become so common, one can only wonder how in the world it got that way.

Not to oversimplify, but I believe I can sum up the answer in one sentence. It is a sentence found inscribed on many store products. It simply says, "FOR BEST RESULTS FOLLOW INSTRUCTIONS OF THE MAKER." God created families, and he left clear, understandable instructions to follow; but many have not done that. For the most part, people have gone their own way and ignored God's directions, and the result has been chaos, pain and devastation in the home.

We must be aware there are some who have tried their very best to make their marriage work, but because their partner did not share their determination and insisted on indulging in harmful behavior, the marriage was doomed for failure. I call these situations, "The Three A's of Divorce: Adultery, Abandonment and Abuse." God's love makes allowance for these extreme situations.

So, what can be done? Is it too late for us? Is it too late for our country? I believe as long as we're alive it is never too late, but there is only one solution - turn back to God! Open the wonderful Holy Bible that has been gathering dust on your shelf. Find all those amazing scriptures that instruct husbands, wives, children, parents, etc. exactly what to do, and just DO IT so your family can be strong and full of love. There is unlimited power for your life in his Word, but only if you *DO* what it says.

PRAYER – Lord, I pray for my family today. Help us each to honor and love one another. Help us to overlook each other's faults and love each other with compassion and patience. I thank you for my family and pray that our lives and love for each other will be an inspiration to others. AMEN

I Love PK's

By Jeri Ingram

I have no greater joy than to hear that
my children are walking in the truth.
3 John 1:4 (NIV)

Years ago, our denomination owned a campground, and
each summer was filled with week-long camps that offered
wonderful Christian fellowship and activities. For several
years in a row, my husband, a long-time pastor in the district,
was asked to preach the PK's Camp, a camp especially for
pastors' teenage kids, or 'PK's as they were affectionately
called. For years we had heard horror stories of how badly
many PK's behaved. Our daughters were young and we
hadn't faced the challenging teenage years yet, so we didn't
know what to expect.

When Camp began, we were stunned to hear teenager after
teenager exclaim, "I hate my church! I hate God! I hate the
ministry!" They complained that their parents had given all
or most of their time, energy and attention to their ministry
and church, leaving their teens to feel like outsiders.

My husband desperately wanted to change that, so he gave
the kids a mantra that became the driving theme of every
PK Camp we held. Over & over, he had them shout, *I AM*

SOMEBODY! He had them open every meeting with that shout, and he would stop at different times throughout his sermon and have them shout it again. He was determined, with God's help, to help them realize they were important to the Kingdom of God. We were blessed to see many of those precious PK's come to the altar, weeping before God, and many responding to the call of God on their lives. It was beautiful!

That experience was such an eye opener to us. We knew we had to take action to prevent our own daughters from falling into that same trap, so once we got home we asked God to give us a plan. We believed our daughters were our most prized possession and the only thing on earth that we could take to Heaven with us, so we were determined that Satan would not steal their destiny.

The plan God gave us was simple; basically two-fold. First, we would make sure to spend plenty of time with our girls by scheduling time on our calendar for them. Weekly family nights were a must and could only be canceled by death or an extreme emergency in the church.

Second, we determined to include our girls in the ministry with us. They loved it and so did we. My husband was always able to find age-appropriate things for them to do, and as they grew and matured, their giftings began to emerge because they were active and involved in the church.

In addition, when we received calls from people with prayer requests, we would all four gather together and pray. We made sure our girls knew their prayers were just as meaningful to God as ours.

The plan was simple yet effective. We were consistent through their growing up years, and today, many years later, we are enjoying the fruits of it. They are still serving God today – they love the church, they love God, and they love the ministry. To us, there is no greater blessing!

No matter what your ministry or career, I would encourage you to remember that your greatest ministry is to your children. Make time for them. Make sure they know how important they are to you, and how important they are to God. God chose you to be the one to shape and mold them into beautiful vessels to be used by God. No one else can do it like you, and the years you have with them are short and fast, and then you are done. Don't waste that time! There is truly no greater joy you can have than to know that your children are walking successfully in the truth of God.

PRAYER – Lord, help me to start today making up for any time I may have lost in raising up my child in a strong and godly way. Give me a plan to follow to help them fulfill their destiny. Give me the right words to encourage and inspire them to live God's perfect will for their lives. AMEN

Don't Go To Bed Mad

By Jeri Ingram

> Don't sin by letting anger control you. Don't
> let the sun go down while you are still
> angry, for anger gives a foothold to the devil.
> Ephesians 4:26 (NLT)

It happened many years ago, but it seems like just yesterday. My husband and I were young and our two daughters were just toddlers.

One night we had an argument about something. I don't even remember what it was about, but I just couldn't seem to get over it. I felt hurt and angry. What made it worse was that he didn't even seem to realize I was still upset. He calmly went to bed without me and quickly fell asleep. I was still up, and still furious, so I went into the kitchen and loudly washed and dried dishes, hoping to wake him, but it didn't work!

I finally gave up and went to bed, turning my back to him, of course, but as I laid there steaming, a scripture began to roll around in my mind. I remembered that the Lord cautioned people not to go to bed mad. He wanted things worked out before they went to sleep to prevent poisonous anger from festering in the heart that would create insurmountable barriers in the relationship.

I knew God was speaking to me and, more than anything, I wanted to be obedient, but I just didn't know what to do with the overwhelming anger, hurt and emotion I was feeling. And besides, my husband was still blissfully sleeping, so what was I to do? I was still mad, and I wanted to wake him, so I did the only logical thing I could think of --- I kicked him!

Well, that certainly got his attention. He sat straight up in bed, stunned, and exclaimed, "What was that for?" I piously replied, "YOU are making me sin!"

After a moment of confused silence, he asked, "What in the world are you talking about?" I replied even more piously, "God said don't let the sun go down on your wrath and you are letting me do just that."

After another moment of stunned silence, he suddenly burst into loud laughter saying, "Jeri, that is the wildest thing I have ever heard." He was laughing so hard that it made me start laughing. We both laid there laughing till we were exhausted, then we kissed and hugged. The argument was over.

I admit it was definitely not the best action on my part, and I certainly don't recommend kicking your spouse, but I believe God saw the desire of my heart and He honored that.

Don't be afraid to step out in obedience even if you don't know exactly how to do it. God will help you. What a loving, caring, and generous God we serve!

PRAYER – Lord, help me today to be obedient to you in every situation. Even during those times when I don't feel like it and don't know exactly what to do, remind me of your grace and help in times of need. AMEN

It's Not A Cliche — God Really Does Answer Prayer

By Jeri Ingram

The prayer of a righteous person is powerful
and effective. James 5:16 (NIV)

One day our daughter came home from school announcing she didn't want to ever go back! When I questioned her, I learned that her kindergarten music class was studying music from the rock group, "Kiss". The teacher even showed the album covers that depicted the singers spitting blood. Our daughter was terrified and I was heartsick. This was not what we were sending our children to school to learn.

Another time, our other daughter came home from school stating that her math teacher had announced to the class that she would use a decapitator on anyone who missed the math question posted on the chalk board. The teacher was brandishing a long, metal pointer as she made the foreboding announcement. Again, our daughter was nervous to go back to school.

That was it! I had had it! Incidents like this kept happening, and I simply had to find a school with a more wholesome atmosphere. I asked my husband if he would mind putting the girls to bed that night so I could have time to pray -- I desperately needed to hear from God! So that night after supper, he took the girls to get them ready for bed and I went into another room, closed the door, and went to prayer. All night long I cried out to God for a solution, and I didn't come out of that room till 8:00 am the next morning!

When I came out of my prayer room, my husband, who was as disturbed as I, looked at me and said, "OK, you have done your part, now I'm going to do mine", and he got into the car and started driving. For several days, he just drove and drove all around the area, stopping at gas stations, convenience stores, talking to people, asking if anyone knew of a Christian school in the area.

Back then, the Christian-school movement was just beginning, and there were very few Christian schools in existence, however, I trusted God would help us.

Finally, it happened! My husband found someone who knew of one forty miles away. We immediately made an appointment and met with the principal where we learned they had just two openings left! We knew those spots were just for our girls! Once again God proved that He answers prayer.

If you have a need, no matter how desperate or helpless it seems, cry out to God for help. He is always faithful to answer!

PRAYER - Lord, there is nothing on this earth more powerful than praying to the one true God! Please remind me, every time I am in trouble, to cry out to you in prayer! Your love for us is demonstrated every time you answer our prayers, and I thank you with all my heart. You are a good God, and I thank you for watching over my life. AMEN

Are Your Children Growing Bitter Or Better?

By Jeri Ingram

Train up a child in the way he should go and
when he is old, he will not depart from it.
Proverbs 22:6 (KJV)

Most Christian schools are wonderful because Christ is honored there, but they are not perfect because human beings are there.

One of the students in our daughters' small Christian school was a young girl whose father was a pastor in a different denomination than ours. The young girl had been taught to be very prejudiced against other denominations and she began to talk against our daughters as soon as they arrived. She was negative and forceful and before long had convinced the whole student body of 30 students that our daughters' church was some kind of cult. When we would drive up to pick them up after school, all the children would be at one end of the school yard playing together, while our two daughters were at the opposite end alone.

We were heartbroken. Our church was filled with Christ-honoring and loving people, and we were certainly not part of any cult!

My husband and I asked God for the wisdom to handle things in a way that could be a positive learning experience for our girls. Each day in the car on the way home from school, we would listen sympathetically as they shared the hurts they had experienced that day, then very gently talk to them about how Jesus would handle a situation like that. We shared truths from the Bible, such as:

- A soft answer turneth away wrath. Proverbs 15:1 KJV
- So in everything, do to others what you would have them do to you. Matthew 7:12 NIV
- Be ye kind one to another. Ephesians 4:32 KJV
- Love never fails. I Corinthians 13:8 NIV

Then we prayed with the girls that God would give them the grace and strength to do what the Bible says. Each morning before school we prayed with them, and they would come home each day with stories of how they tried to respond like Jesus would, and gradually, we noticed a change. They seemed stronger and were coming home feeling happier.

One afternoon, as we drove up to the schoolyard, we were surprised to see some of the students playing with our daughters. Each day more and more of the students joined our girls at their end of the schoolyard till they were all there playing together. Sadly, the one girl who had been the instigator never made the change, and she was all alone at the other end. The school children had grown weary of her negative, aggressive behavior and decided they would rather play with our daughters.

What a great opportunity it was for our daughters to learn first-hand that doing things God's way never fails. If we had allowed our emotions to rule, we could have become bitter and angry, and our daughters would have missed the opportunity to learn a valuable life lesson.

When your children face challenges in life, help them avoid the temptation to feel like a victim. Instead, show them Biblical scriptures on being an overcomer; then with love, tenderness, patience and prayer, help them walk through their trials victoriously. It will prepare them for living a victorious, overcoming life as adults!

PRAYER – Lord, give me the grace and wisdom to teach my children the ways of God. Help me to show them how God would want them to handle the difficult situations they will face in life. Make me alert and sensitive to the times they need encouragement and guidance. Thank you for your help in this important task of training my children. AMEN

The Thief Must Restore Seven-fold

By Jeri Ingram

But if he is caught, he must pay back seven
times what he stole. Proverbs 6:31 (NLT)

Many years ago, we were pastoring a church in Pasadena, Texas, a town just outside of Houston. One day we went down the street to have lunch in a café located in the center of the mall. Before we sat down, I draped my wool coat over the back of my chair, and later forgot to take it with me when we left the café. When I realized I had forgotten it, my husband turned and went back quickly to get it, but it was already gone.

At first I was upset, but then I started thinking about the scripture that says, "But if he is caught, he must pay back seven times what he stole." Then I told the Lord that I forgave the person who stole it, and asked the Lord to forgive them. Then I told the Lord that I decided to freely GIVE the coat to that person as a GIFT, and I asked the Lord to let that person FEEL the anointing every time they wore that coat, and to lead them to salvation. It totally set me free from any anger I felt towards that person.

So, instead of feeling angry, I began to feel really happy and excited over how this person was going to get zapped with the anointing every time they put the coat on, and also over the 7-fold return the devil was going to give to me. I thanked God over and over and continued to stand in faith.

And, sure enough! Within just a few weeks I was given a lovely silver fox jacket as a gift! The stolen wool coat had cost me $100, and the silver fox jacket cost a little over $700! My coat was restored – 7-fold!

Please don't misunderstand me. My goal is not to inspire people to just seek after material things. The Lord already told us that if we put him and his Kingdom first in our lives that all our needs will be met. My goal, rather, is to remind people that God is trustworthy, and if he promised it in his Word, it is because he wants us to trust him for it so he can show his goodness to us and how much he loves us.

Our Heavenly Father is faithful to perform his Word! We just have to believe!

PRAYER – Lord, I declare today, by the authority of God's Holy Word, that Satan has to restore everything he has stolen from me and my family, 7-fold! List your stolen items. Satan is a thief and wants to kill, steal and destroy us, but greater is he that is in us than he who is in the world. So, by the grace, and mercy, and power, and authority of our God ---- WE WIN!

Thank you Lord! AMEN

Don't Be Afraid of The Storm!

By Jeri Ingram

> And he arose, and rebuked the wind, and
> said unto the sea, 'Peace, be still'. And the
> wind ceased, and there was a great calm.
> Mark 4:39 (KJV)

Watching the news these days can be nerve wracking. Fighting, anger, and violence erupt every day. Unquenchable fires, mud slides, storms of historic proportions, hurricanes, tornados, earthquakes -- the list is unending. It would be easy for a person to be overcome by fear if your focus is on these things. But if you will look closely at the life of Jesus you will see that, as believers, we can choose a better way. We can choose to reject fear and choose faith in God to protect us through the storms of life.

My husband graduated from Southwestern Assemblies of God University in Waxahachie, Texas. While there, we lived on campus in the trailer park that was designated for married students. The campus itself was nicknamed by the students as "tornado alley". It was common for tornados to blow through there.

One day, we noticed the skies turning very dark with an ominous green color that signified an approaching tornado. We knew our little trailer certainly wasn't the safest place to be, especially with a toddler and an infant, and we knew we had to do something fast! The storm, however, was approaching so quickly that there was no time to go anywhere, so we gathered our babies, huddled in the kitchen, and held hands to pray for safety. As we were praying, the wind was deafening, and suddenly we felt one end of the trailer begin to lift up into the air! It kept slowly lifting, higher and higher, while the whole trailer was shaking violently. We never looked up, we just kept praying!

As we continued praying, we could feel the trailer very slowly settling back down to the ground, and gradually, the wind began to subside. Finally, when we felt it was safe, we went outside to check things out and were amazed to find the trailer had set back down on its blocks with precise accuracy. We knew God had answered our prayers. We couldn't stop thanking and praising Him over and over!

Once again, God proved to us that He is more powerful than any storm we might face here on earth. Even tornados!

We encourage you today to reject fear & choose faith. There will be many challenging things to face in these perilous End Times, but God's Word has promised that if we trust in him, we will overcome them all!!!

PRAYER – Father, I thank you that you promised to take care of your children. Would you watch over my family today, and protect us from the storms of life. We are trusting in you and thank you for your loving care. AMEN

How To Walk In Love When You Don't Feel Like It

By Jeri Ingram

> A new commandment I give unto you, that
> ye love one another; as I have loved you, that
> ye also love one another. By this shall all men
> know that ye are my disciples, if ye have love
> one to another. John 13:34, 35 (KJV)

God commands us to love one another, even though He knew there would be times we would not FEEL like loving. How is that possible? One of the first lessons I learned as a new Christian is that love is a *CHOICE*, a *DECISION*. We *CHOOSE* to walk in love, even when we don't feel like it!

I had only been saved a short while when I was introduced to an older woman in the church who seemed to feel it was her mission in life to make everyone miserable, so everyone avoided her. When I would see her, however, I tried to strike up a conversation and be friendly, but she would immediately let out a barrage of negative, critical, insulting remarks that were very upsetting. Soon, I found myself avoiding her like everyone else.

One night I was at home alone while my husband was at work. As I was sitting in my living room praying, the presence of God became so rich and full, and so powerful that I became overwhelmed with his love, and I started praying, "God, I want to know you more. I want to be more like you. I want to be closer to you. How can I please you more?"

I was groaning from the depths of my heart when I heard the Lord's still, small voice inside my spirit saying, "I want you to call Mrs. Smith (not her real name) and ask her to forgive you for hurting her."

I thought, W-H-A-T!!!!! That couldn't be right! God wouldn't ask me to do that! But he continued to impress upon me to call her. You could have knocked me over with a feather!

I had done nothing but try to be kind and polite to her, and she had done nothing but be rude and insulting to me, and God wanted ME to call HER & apologize. Unbelievable!

So, I argued with Him! I wrestled! I wept! And for over an hour I struggled, until finally I resigned myself to the fact that you just cannot win an argument with God. So reluctantly I said, "Ok, Lord! I'll do it, but I sure don't *FEEL* like it," and instantly I heard the Lord say, "You just obey – I'll take care of the feelings."

Slowly, I went over and picked up the phone and started dialing. My hands were trembling with emotion because I *DID NOT* want to do this, but as I dialed, something unexpected began happening to me. I felt a warm and smooth feeling begin to spread over me, starting at the top of my head and flowing to the soles of my feet. It felt like I was being enveloped with "liquid love" from God.

By the time the woman answered the phone, I actually felt such an incredible love for her that I knew only God himself could have put it there. With earnest sincerity, I said to her, "If I've hurt you in any way, would you please forgive me?" Dead silence! So I waited, and after a moment I began to hear sniffling. When she finally spoke, she quietly thanked me and said no one had ever talked to her like that before.

From that day on she was different. She became friendly and pleasant. My act of obedience to God had set her free. And it set me free, as well. I learned that day that obedience to God has absolutely nothing to do with how I feel. When we CHOOSE to obey, God comes on the scene with grace and love to help us.

Try it yourself. Decide to walk in love. Tell your spouse "I love you", even when you don't *FEEL* like it, & watch your marriage begin to blossom once again, like a beautiful flower after it has received a drink of cool, fresh water. Serving God is the most marvelous thing*!*

PRAYER – Father, help me today to walk in love with my family, with my co-workers, and with my neighbors and friends. Help me remember that I am an Ambassador for Christ, shedding his love abroad everywhere I go. This world is hurting and is so in need of God's love. Remind me daily that showing love is a CHOICE, a DECISION that only I can make. Thank you for your help. AMEN

A Gift For Angel

By Jeri Ingram

Each of you should give you what you have
decided in your heart to give, not reluctantly
or under compulsion, for God loves a cheerful
giver. 2 Corinthians 9:7 (NIV)

We had recently moved back to Texas from New England and were staying with my husband's parents until we could find a house to buy. I had been trying to save enough money for a down payment. Using a shoe box, I put every spare cent in it, but I had only managed to save $300. At this rate, I thought, it will take me twenty or thirty years to get enough money together just for a down payment.

That week we had a special speaker coming to speak to our church. His name was Angel. He was a tiny little man, less than 5 feet tall, who pastored a church in Mexico. Our church had been installing water wells for some of the villages there, and he was coming to our church to thank our people for all the help. As I was at home that afternoon, Angel's face began to appear before me. I suddenly saw myself laying my shoe box of money at Angel's feet, and I knew God was telling me to sow it as a seed for the home we so desperately needed.

I confess that for a moment I struggled. I had worked so hard to save that money, and the thought of starting back at square one was daunting. But then I quickly reminded myself that $300 wasn't going to help us much anyway, and we would be far better off to just trust God to help us.

So, that night I went to church clutching my shoe box. I was filled with excitement! As Angel finished preaching, people were coming forward to the altars to pray, so I stood up and walked forward to the platform. I knelt and placed the shoe box on the first step, then returned to my seat, my heart pounding with anticipation.

A short time later that month, a teacher from the Christian school where I was working called and said they were moving and needed to sell their house and wondered if we might be interested. We met her the next day for a tour of the house, and it was exactly what we wanted and needed. Then she blew us away when she said they were willing to finance it themselves with *NO DOWN PAYMENT*! We cried tears of joy, knowing it was the harvest from the shoebox seed we had sown. Once again, God proved his faithfulness.

PRAYER – Lord, thank you for your faithfulness. Thank you for caring about our needs; thank you for loving us enough to show us how to sow seeds into the Kingdom. Your ways are so far above ours. We trust you with our lives and all we have. Everything we have comes from you, and it is with joyful and grateful hearts that we give unto you. AMEN

Don't Make It About You!

By Jeri Ingram

> If their children are honored, they do not
> know it; if their offspring are brought low,
> they do not see it. They feel but the pain
> of their own bodies and mourn only for
> themselves. Job 14: 21-22 (NIV)

A lot of adults are walking around in utter selfishness. They see nothing but their own problems and they are so self-centered and self-focused that they spend most of their lives feeling sorry for themselves when they could be experiencing tremendous joy by influencing the next generation.

One time a man asked me how to relate to his son. He was frustrated because he wanted to play sports with him, but the son loved computers and did not enjoy sports. The dad couldn't understand why the son didn't want to be with him, but it was obvious that it was because the dad was more interested in what was fun for *HIMSELF* than for his son. Ask the CHILD what THEY would enjoy doing if you want them to enjoy their time spent with you.

Our son-in-law, Tim, illustrated this perfectly several years ago when his children were much younger. One Saturday morning, he went dirt bike riding with his teenage son,

Cody. Then later that same day he had a tea party with his young daughter, Kaylee. Talk about diversity! When talking about it later, you could tell my son-in-law enjoyed each activity equally. I'm pretty sure it wasn't the actual tea party that he found so enjoyable. It was spending time with his daughter in a way that she was able to relate and enjoy! He found a way to spend time with each child, doing something that was meaningful to each. That is the kind of quality time that builds strong bonds between parents and children.

We have a choice! We can live joyful lives by focusing on others, or we can lead miserable lives by focusing on ourselves.

PRAYER – Lord, give me understanding and insight today regarding the needs of my family. Help me to lay aside my own personal desires and focus on what would help my children to realize how valuable they are to me and to God. Make our time today special and memorable, so they can look back on wonderful memories. AMEN

The Next Generation Needs A Moral Compass

By Jeri Ingram

"Take on an entirely new way of life, a God-
fashioned life renewed from the inside and
working itself into your conduct as God
accurately reproduces His character in you."
Ephesians 4: 23-24 (The Message)

Character is a word that describes morals and ethics and integrity. It's being the right kind of person and doing the right thing, even in difficult situations. Trying to live without character is like using a map of Texas to find your way around Massachusetts. Every decision you make will be wrong!

I find that many in this younger generation don't know right from wrong today. It is heartbreaking! One day I was at the store getting my cell phone repaired. The young man waiting on me was well dressed, clean cut, very pleasant and polite, and a pleasure to work with. But while he was working on my phone, he kept nervously glancing at his own cell phone lying next to him on the counter.

Finally, he apologized for looking at it so often. He said, "I'm sorry I keep looking at my phone, but my girlfriend is due to have our baby any minute and I'm trying to stay in touch."

You could visibly see his excitement and anticipation. I was glad I was wearing my sunglasses because tears instantly sprang to my eyes as I thought about that helpless, innocent little baby growing up with the life-long stigma of being illegitimate. Even if the parents do eventually get married, the baby's birth certificate and the parent's marriage certificate will forever reveal the truth --- the baby was conceived out of wedlock. The Bible says that is not God's plan. His plan is for a couple to marry first, *then* have children. That creates a good foundation for a family to build upon the rest of their lives.

It's important for the next generation to know how to make a living, but it's even more important for them to know how to LIVE! If you're a parent, teach your children the scripture: "a wise person is hungry for knowledge while the fool feeds on trash". Proverbs 15:14 (NLT). In our modern-day language we could say … GARBAGE IN – GARBAGE OUT!

We must find a way to reach this next generation before it's too late, because the enemy is at the gate!

PRAYER –Lord, this generation desperately needs to know the love of God! I pray that you would move in a special way to reach them and touch them by the power of your Holy Spirit. AMEN

The Crash Program

By Jeri Ingram

> Fathers, do not provoke your children to
> anger (do not exasperate them to the point
> of resentment with demands that are trivial
> or unreasonable or humiliating or abusive;
> nor by showing favoritism or indifference to
> any of them), but bring them up (tenderly,
> with loving kindness) in the discipline and
> instruction of the Lord. Ephesians 6:4 (AMP)

When you're raising your children, don't be overly harsh and critical. It can cause them to become bitter and resentful, and in extreme cases it can even break their spirits.

But neither should you be too permissive. Children need proper boundaries, or they can become involved in harmful behavior to themselves or to others. God is kind, but He is not soft! He knows all too well that the wages of sin is death, so He expects parents to care enough about their children to hold them accountable for their actions.

You could say true love is like a two-sided coin. One side shows love, affirmation and nurturing, while the other side gives correction, instruction and accountability. For a coin to have one side without the other side would be an incomplete coin – a phony. The same is true with true love.

To love without discipline or to discipline without love — either way would be equally harmful, not true love.

Although they would never admit it, children and teenagers alike WANT BOUNDARIES! It gives them a sense of safety and security, and they instinctively know it's your job as parents to provide those boundaries. When you make excuses for their wrong actions, and don't enforce proper behavior, they lose respect for you.

When our daughters were small, my husband and I designed a program of discipline for them that was very effective. We called it "The Crash Program". If we noticed their behavior was getting 'off track' in some way, we notified each other and immediately "The Crash Program" went into effect. Each time, we would sit down with our girls and explain what we were doing and why. Actions that we might normally overlook because they seemed so small were not overlooked. We brought them to accountability on every little thing —- *big or small* -- and applied appropriate discipline and correction. In short, we cracked down!

At the same time, we did something else that we felt was equally important. Since we were intensifying our watchful attitude of correction and discipline, we equally intensified our attitude of love and affirmation. For every word or action of discipline, we made sure there was an equal word or gesture of love and acceptance. Every time we walked by them, we would give them a loving pat or hug and verbally reminded them how much we loved them. We made it abundantly clear that, even though they must accept responsibility and proper punishment for their wrong actions, there was nothing they could do that would cause us to stop loving them. We showed them unconditional love, just the way our Heavenly Father does for us.

The reward we received for that effort was immeasurable. As parents, we never experienced the heartbreak and stress of teenage rebellion. Our daughters matured with grace and speed. Even when we asked our oldest daughter to refrain for a while from dating a young man in whom she was obviously very interested because he was a new Christian and we wanted to make sure of the stability of his walk with the Lord, she never rebelled.

She obeyed her father's wishes, and you can't imagine her joy when, a year later, her dad approved the young man and gave her permission to begin dating him. They eventually married and have blessed us with three beautiful grandchildren. Now married over twenty years, Kimberly's husband, Tom, is like a son to us, and we can't imagine life without him. Our youngest daughter, Kristina, also married a wonderful young man, Tim, and he, too, is like a son to us, and they have blessed us with two beautiful grandchildren.

The blessings that come into your lives as you do your best to follow his instructions written in his Word are greater than anything you could ever imagine.

PRAYER – Lord, I thank you for the beautiful children and grandchildren with which you have blessed us. I pray that you will help us to always find the proper balance between loving them and giving them Godly discipline.

Help me to never break their spirits by being overly harsh and demanding, and help me never be so permissive they feel their actions don't have consequences. Help me to be the parent you desire me to be, in the mighty name of Jesus! – AMEN

Follow Peace!

By Jeri Ingram

Let the peace of Christ rule in your hearts.
Colossians 3:15 (NIV)

9/11 is a day that is burned into the memory of all Americans. I am sure most people can remember every detail of that fateful day.

For several weeks prior to that day my husband and I had been preparing to take a trip to North Carolina where our daughter and her family lived for several years before returning to New England. My husband had planned to call the airlines to purchase our tickets, but for some reason he kept putting it off. Every day I asked him if he had gotten the tickets and every day he said, "Oh, I'm sorry, I forgot. I'll do it tomorrow".

After a while I began to express my frustration, but he continued to procrastinate day after day. Finally, one day my husband looked at me with a perplexed look and said, "Honestly, I don't know why I haven't called for the tickets, but I just can't seem to make myself do it.'

For a long time we had always tried to find God's direction by allowing his peace to lead us. If we didn't feel peace, we didn't do it. We felt that lack of peace was God's way of keeping us on a safe path, so after discussing the situation and praying about it, we decided that God must be saying, "Don't fly", so we decided to drive.

Early the morning of September 10, 2001, we got into our car and began the long drive to North Carolina, still wondering why the Lord had stopped us from travelling by air, which would have been so much faster! Later on, we stopped at a motel for the night somewhere between Boston and Charlotte.

The next morning, we were getting dressed in our motel room when the unbelievable news came over the TV that an airplane had crashed into the Twin Towers in New York City! We were shocked, and we hurriedly dressed and left the hotel so we could continue hearing the news report on the car radio.

Driving down the highway, hearing report after report, it finally came clear that the crash was no accident. America was under attack by terrorists! We were stunned! As the realization of the unthinkable began to sink into our dazed minds, we suddenly realized that this atrocity was happening at the very time we would have been flying out of Boston. We learned later that all flights were cancelled, and some friends of ours who were scheduled to fly out of Boston that same morning wound up sitting in the airport all day long. They said it was chaotic and nerve wracking!

Dick's obedience to the Lord kept us from being in the middle of that chaos. God protected us, even though we did not understand what was happening or why! I felt overwhelmed with gratitude to the Lord and to my husband. I couldn't stop hugging him and kissing his face and thanking him for being such a good husband and ignoring my protests!

That incident is a continual reminder to me to allow peace to rule and guide me in every situation, whether I understand what is happening or not. God is all-knowing and He can protect us from dangers that we don't even know are coming!

FOLLOW PEACE!!!

PRAYER--Lord, I thank you with all my heart for your loving care and guidance. You promised to never leave us and you would always watch over us. Help me to listen and be sensitive to your voice and to allow the peace of God to lead and guide me every day of my life, and I will give you all the praise and glory! AMEN

Be Imitators Of God

By Jeri Ingram

> Therefore, become imitators of God (copy
> Him and follow His example), as well-
> beloved children (imitate their father).
> Ephesians 5:1 (Amp)

The Bible clearly tells us that God rewards his children for seeking and obeying him. The Bible also tells us to imitate him the way little children sometimes like to imitate their parents.

My nephew, David, is a grown man now, but when he was just a tiny tot, barely able to walk, he used to love to imitate his dad. Sometimes his dad would lean his back against the wall with his legs crossed and his hands in his pockets. Then we would look down and there would be my nephew, David, right beside him − leaning back against the wall with legs crossed and hands in his pockets. Of course, his little legs were so short he would sometimes just fall over on the ground, but he gave it his most valiant effort. He was determined to imitate his dad whom he obviously adored.

That is what God wants from us, his dear children, to read his Word to see what God is like and how he acts, and then give our most valiant effort to imitate that. Even if we 'fall over' sometimes because of our human failings, we never stop trying. He is our Heavenly Father that we adore, so we spend a lifetime learning how to be like him. What joy!

PRAYER. Lord, help me today to be more like you. In every situation I encounter, show me what you would say and how you would respond. Then give me the grace to imitate you. You are my supreme example, so help me give my most valiant effort to imitate you. AMEN

Rewards Are Wonderful!

By Jeri Ingram

... God is a rewarder of those who earnestly
and diligently seek Him. Hebrews 11:6 (AMP)

We started teaching our daughters about the Lord when
they were tiny. When they were three years old, they could
each name all 66 books of the Bible by memory, as well as
many scripture verses.

To accomplish this, we hung a large poster on their bedroom
door. On the top half of the poster was written all the books
of the Bible and on the bottom half we listed each scripture
as they memorized it. Each time they learned a new book
or a new scripture, they got a gold star beside it. Every time
they accumulated ten gold stars, we took them to the local
dime store and let them pick out a prize. Their excitement
was a joy to watch, and the prizes motivated them to keep
on learning. They loved the prizes and were proud of their
accomplishments. That knowledge built a strong foundation
into their lives that is still with them today.

One time a lady told me we were wrong to do that. She
said it was like bribery and they should learn to do it just
because it is the right thing to do. I respectfully disagreed

and reminded her that scripture says that God is a rewarder, and we are instructed to imitate His example.

Our daughters are now married and are passing to their own children the valuable Bible knowledge they learned when they were young. We are amazed at how much our grandchildren have learned at their young ages.

Thank God we serve a loving God who cares about us enough to reward us when we are endeavoring to seek him and learn more about him and his wonderful ways! I would like to challenge parents to find creative ways to reward their own children, and watch them thrive and blossom as they grow into mature and responsible adults. There is no greater blessing!

PRAYER – Lord, I thank you that you love us enough to motivate us to seek you by rewarding us. Help us to be good and godly parents by rewarding our own children in the same way so they will be motivated to learn about this great and wonderful God we serve. AMEN

God's Bailout Plan

By Jeri Ingram

Give and it shall be given unto you, good
measure, pressed down, shaken together, and
running over shall men give into your bosom.
For with what measure you give, it shall be
measured to you again. Luke 6:38 (KJV)

I'm sure you all remember a few years ago when the
government came up with a creative solution to our
nation's financial problems called the Bailout Plan. You
also probably remember that it didn't work out so well. I
remember hearing reports of one bad situation after another
on the news during that time. I kept thinking, "God has
financial strategies for his children that never fail, we should
call it God's Bailout Plan."

When God created the universe he set numerous laws into
motion, both natural laws and spiritual laws that are still
in operation today. The law of gravity is a natural law that
keeps our feet firmly planted on the ground. The law of
'giving and receiving', is a spiritual law from God where
he has promised if we give generously with a pure heart,
he will give back to us in amazing abundance. Farmers call
this the law of sowing and reaping and they understand this
principle better than anyone. If they don't continue planting

good seeds into good soil season after season, guess what will happen! No crops!

The first time I ever experienced this spiritual law working in my life was many years ago after my husband and I had just moved from Texas to New England to pioneer a new church. I was born and raised in Texas, and all my clothes were designed for summer, totally inadequate for a New England winter, and I was freezing! I only owned one boot-length skirt, and because we were pioneer pastors starting a brand-new church, I did not have the money to go shopping, so I went to prayer.

I specifically asked the Lord if he would provide me with some warm, boot-length skirts. Instantly, I heard his still, small voice inside me say, "plant a seed"! I had never heard anyone say that before and I did not know exactly what it meant. When I asked the Lord to clarify, I began to picture in my mind the face of a lady in our church. I immediately understood he was telling me to give my one long skirt to that particular woman as an act of faith.

Immediately, I put the skirt in a bag and placed it in the trunk of my car so I would not be tempted to change my mind. The next Sunday I took it into church and gave it to her. She looked so surprised and pleased. I explained that I was planting a seed in obedience to the Lord's instructions. Remarkably, over the next few months, people who had no knowledge of my prayer for winter clothes, or the seed I had sown, gifted me a total of nine beautiful, warm, boot-length skirts!

That was my first experience of operating within God's financial laws. Since that time I have seen this law in action over and over! Man's plans will fail, but God's plans will never fail!

PRAYER – Lord, I thank you for your provision for your children. I thank you that even when the world-systems are failing, you never fail! Help us remember when we are facing difficult times that *we can never out give you.* You are always generous and care about our every need. We thank you with all our hearts for being such a loving, caring Heavenly Father. AMEN

Live The Life Before Them

By Jeri Ingram

> Amaziah did what was pleasing in the Lord's
> sight, but not like his ancestor David. Instead,
> he followed the example of his father, Joash.
> Amaziah did not destroy the pagan shrines,
> and the people still offered sacrifices and
> burned incense there. 2 Kings 14:3,4 (NLT)

One time I read a story about a man who got so mad at his wife that he exploded and pounded the table yelling, "I hate you! I won't take it anymore! No, no, no!"

Sometime later he heard noises from his two-year-old son's room. When he went down to check, he got chills down his spine when he heard that two-year-old repeating word for word, with the same exact voice inflections, what his dad had said to his mom earlier. "I hate you! I won't take it anymore! No, no, no!"

The man realized in shock and horror that he had passed his own pain, anger and unforgiveness on to the NEXT GENERATION!

How do we instead make sure that the truths of God are passed on from generation to generation? We must teach them with our words and consistently LIVE those convictions! They must be modeled by our lives! In fact, if we don't live that life in front of them, our words will have no meaning.

As the saying goes, "our actions speak louder than our words"! Ask God to give you the grace and strength to live your life in a way that your children can safely follow your example.

PRAYER – Lord, help me to live my life in such a way that my children will be inspired to live for God. Help me to let my light shine in my own home. By your grace, Lord, let my children see the love and grace of God demonstrated through my life in a way that will cause them to desire to serve God throughout their lifetime. AMEN

God Should Be
Represented Correctly

By Jeri Ingram

But Jesus said, suffer the little children,
and forbid them not to come unto me:
for of such is the Kingdom of Heaven.
Matthew 19:14 (KJV)

During the years we pastored, my husband always loved to keep a bowl of candy on his desk and continually invited the children to help themselves. He did that because he felt it is the job of the pastor to represent God in the right way to the people, especially the children. He felt it was one way to show the children that God loves them and wants to give them gifts. It presented God to them as a Heavenly Father who cares about them.

One day we learned the children had been told by some misguided person in the church they were no longer allowed to come into Pastor's office. We were so upset! We felt it sent a a HUGE message to the children that God was no longer interested in them, and he no longer had time for them. When Jesus was on earth, the Bible says he was greatly displeased when the disciples kept the children from coming to him, and we felt the same way!

We immediately went to work to try to correct the situation. Every time we saw a child in the hallway, we invited them into the office to get a piece of candy. When they came in, they also got hugs as a reminder of God's love and acceptance.

I will never forget the day four or five little girls came in to get a piece of candy. They were all laughing and talking and were so adorable. I playfully told them they came at exactly the right time because we were just starting to form "THE MOST BEAUTIFUL GIRLS IN THE WORLD CLUB", & they were the perfect girls to be the charter members. They just beamed! I said that to them because Jesus said "suffer the little children, & forbid them not to come unto me: for of such is the Kingdom of Heaven." God loves little children and he wants us to demonstrate that to them in a way to which they can relate.

God expects to be represented to his people in the right way, and children are the most impressionable and vulnerable of all. Ask God to help you be alert and aware of the needs of the children with which you come in contact each day. A smile or a kind word might be the very thing they need to lift their spirits. Let God's love shine through you into their hearts. It could make all the difference!

PRAYER – Lord, I pray that you will make me always mindful of the needs of my children, and every child with whom I come in contact. Children are precious to you, and they should be precious to us as well. Help me to demonstrate to them by my words and actions that God loves them and they are extremely valuable in His sight. AMEN

Empowered To Witness

By Jeri Ingram

> But you shall receive power, after that the
> Holy Ghost is come upon you; and ye shall
> be witnesses unto me both in Jerusalem, and
> in all Judea, and in Samaria, and unto the
> uttermost parts of the earth. Acts 1:8 (KJV)

My husband and I were both saved and baptized in the Holy Spirit one week apart. We both had powerful experiences, and our lives were impacted in ways we could never have foreseen. It felt like fire was shut up in our bones & all we wanted to do was tell people what God had done for us.

One of the first decisions we made as new, Spirit-filled believers was to set aside one night a week to invite our friends, one couple at a time, to our home for dinner so we could tell them our story. We were so excited we could not wait to witness to them what Christ had done for us. We did that for a whole year, and during that time we had the thrill of leading several of our friends and relatives to the Lord!

Another time my husband sat down and wrote out his full testimony – eight pages long! I typed it up on pastel blue paper with beautiful white flowers on the heading. We mailed out over 300 copies! The wonderful, positive response we received was a great encouragement. Actually, his first invitation to preach came from a pastor in a neighboring town who read the testimony. Someone in the pastor's congregation gave it to him and said, "You should read this". He did, and immediately called my husband to come and preach in his church. That was the beginning of our ministry, over fifty years ago.

One decision we made that literally changed the direction of our lives was to join with my sister, Maggie, who had started a youth prayer meeting at my parents' home every Friday night. We were still in the Methodist church at that time and we were stunned at the crowds of young people that came week after week. They were so hungry and many of them got saved and filled with the Holy Spirit. It was obviously a sovereign move of God through the youth.

In our youthful naivety we mistakenly thought the pastor would be thrilled to see the young people of his church getting on fire for God! After just a few short months, however, we received a visit from the pastor offering us the 'boot'. We were no longer welcome in our lifelong church where we had grown up. He did not want the Pentecostal experience infiltrating his establishment.

It was sad to leave so many lifelong friends behind, but we believed that God was directing our lives, and He certainly was! He directed us to an Assemblies of God church where we met people who shared our excitement over the obvious move of God happening throughout the south at that time. One of the most heartwarming experiences I had was at the reception following my mother's funeral. There were over 200 relatives and friends in the room, all standing around visiting. I had not seen my cousin, Cathy, for several years and she came up behind me and began to whisper in my ear.

She said, "Look around you, Jeri. Almost every person in this room has become a born-again believer, and it all started when we saw the Holy Spirit sweep through your family, and it caused a hunger to grow in our hearts that set us each on a mission to discover what you had so obviously found!"

That took my breath away!

The Bible clearly promises that receiving the Holy Spirit would empower us to be witnesses. That should be an encouragement to all of us. We don't have to do it in our own strength. The Holy Ghost comes on the scene and produces results we could never produce on our own.

PRAYER – Lord, I thank you for the wonderful infilling of your Holy Spirit. I pray you will lead and guide me to people who are hungry to know you and empower me to witness to them. Give me the right words and let your love shine through me to a world that is hurting and dying. Thank you for the privilege of being a witness for you. AMEN

Don't Harm God's Church!

By Jeri Ingram

If anyone destroys God's temple, God will
destroy that person; for God's temple is
sacred, and you together are that temple.
I Corinthians 3:17 (NIV)

Upon graduation from Southwestern Assemblies of God University, we went to our first place of ministry in our hometown of Houston, Texas. My husband served there as a young, enthusiastic and energetic associate pastor. The senior pastor had faithfully served that church for many years. He was an older man, approaching retirement, and we were looking forward to gleaning from his years of experience.

We had only been serving there a short time when one of the deacons called my husband and invited him to lunch. My husband thought the lunch was an opportunity to get acquainted, but they had barely started eating when the deacon began sharing that he and a few other deacons wanted my husband to replace the senior pastor who was getting older. They wanted to force the senior pastor out and have my husband take his place.

My husband was stunned! It was unthinkable that the deacons were going behind the pastor's back in such an insidious way. He left the restaurant as quickly as possible, and when he arrived home, he shared with me what had happened.

We prayed together for guidance on how to handle it, as we really didn't know what to do! If we stayed, it would cause division in the church; if we left, it would be hurtful to the pastor. My husband decided to make an appointment to see one of the district officials of our denomination, who was also an elder in our church. His advice was startling!

With urgency the official said, "Get out of town! Now! Leave quickly! Don't even explain why because it will be a discouragement to both the senior pastor and the congregation. Just pack up your things and go! You don't want it on your conscience that you helped to force a faithful pastor out of office prematurely and caused strife and division to enter the church."

So, we left! It was hard to leave without saying goodbye to the people, but we knew it was necessary. Looking back, we are so grateful for the wise advice from an elder who understood how important it is to protect the church and the pastor God placed there.

Every pastor will move, resign or retire at some time in their lives, but that timing should be determined by God, and his replacement should be chosen by God. It is God's church, and he should be allowed to make those decisions.

PRAYER – Lord, I pray for my church today and also for my pastor. Protect them from immature Christians, or from preachers with selfish ambition who care more about themselves than they do about the Kingdom of God! Stop anyone who would, knowingly or unknowingly, harm God's church, and let a spirit of love, peace and harmony rule and reign in our hearts. AMEN

Call It In!

By Jeri Ingram

God, who quickens the dead & calls those
things which are not as though they were.
Romans 4:17 (KJV)

We were pastoring a church in our hometown of Pasadena,
Texas, just outside of Houston. Our daughters were teenagers
and were very involved in school and church activities, and
my husband was very busy with his church schedule. At that
time, we only had one car, so it was difficult for each of us
to get to all the places we needed to go.

I began to pray about it because I felt that having another car
would help relieve the pressure on my husband of getting
our daughters to their events. As I prayed, I felt assurance
from the Lord that it was His will to give me a car and I was
to "call it in", according to Romans 4:17 KJV.

I knew the Bible says, "God calls those things which are not
as though they were." (Romans 4:17 KJV), and I knew God
told us to "be imitators of God as dear children" (Ephesians
5:1 NKJV), so I felt He had given me specific instructions
on how to exercise my faith for this endeavor. He wanted me
to call my car out of the supernatural realm into the natural
realm. Some people might think that sounds strange, but

I have always believed that the supernatural realm is more real than this natural realm in which we live. After all, it was the supernatural realm where God dwells that existed long before we did, and he spoke our natural realm into existence. When our natural world passes away and is gone, the spiritual realm will continue to live on for eternity!

For several years my husband and I had been getting exercise by walking around the large high school football field just down the street from our house. As we walked, we prayed, and I began "calling in" a car during our prayer time. Each day I would look up at the sky and call a car, in the mighty name of Jesus, to come to me, and my husband would agree with me. Day after day and week after week we did that.

A couple of months went by, and one day, as we were walking and praying as usual, I looked up at the sky and prayed again for a car. Suddenly, as I was looking at the sky, I saw it! I guess you would call it a vision, but it was a car for sure. It was blue and it was beautiful, and it was driving straight towards me. I knew God had heard my prayers and had answered them. I knew the car was mine, and even though it wasn't there yet in the natural, I knew it was mine by faith. My hands shot straight up in the air, and I began praising God and crying and rejoicing all at the same time!!!!

One week later, my husband was in a meeting with our church board members. We had never said a word about needing a car to anyone, but during the meeting it was suggested that our family needed more than one car and they felt they should buy one for us. They voted unanimously to do just that. Within just a few days, I was driving home in a lovely blue Buick. My heart just overflowed with gratitude that such a great, magnificent God would care about our needs in such a practical way!

I believe God feels that way about *ALL* his children and is just waiting for *ALL* of us to trust him with every need we have in our lives.

PRAYER – Lord, I pray that you would remind me when I forget it is your will to provide for your children, and that our responsibility is to call those things that are not as though they already are. That's how God's chosen people can not only have our own needs met, but also how we can make a difference in the world around us. Help me to be a world changer by calling things from the supernatural realm into the natural realm, to the glory and honor of our God. AMEN

You Reap What You Sow

By Jeri Ingram

Do not be deceived, God is not mocked; for
whatever a man sows, that he will also reap!
Galatians 6:7 (NKJV)

As born-again believers, sometimes we forget that we have the God-given power, ability and responsibility to sow good seeds into others. We sow those seeds by the words we say, the actions we perform, and the decisions we make.

The most important place of all for us to sow those seeds are into our children so that we can pass our faith in God to the next generation. We see that principle in 2 Timothy 1:5 (NIV) where Paul said to Timothy, "I am reminded of your sincere faith, which first lived in your grandmother Lois and in your mother Eunice, and I am persuaded, now lives in you also." And because we are now living in the End Times, there has never been a time where children have more desperately needed parents and grandparents to live a godly example.

When sowing seeds, it is important to pay attention to both the type of seed as well as the quantity of seed. Apple seeds will not produce cucumbers, and seeds of anger and unforgiveness will not produce love and peace. Neither will one little seed produce a large crop. *Generosity is the key!* Simply stated, you reap what you sow – both in quantity and quality.

My mother was a woman of faith, in fact, she was a spark— so full of life, energy and fun! All of my childhood and teenage years she continually planted seeds of faith, hope and love into me. Each month when the Guideposts Magazine arrived, she handed it to me and encouraged me to read the inspiring stories found there. Other times she would challenge me to memorize scriptures within a certain period of time, like the 23rd Psalm. Still another time, she asked me to join her in a special project where we read Psalm 100 seven times a day for seven days. It was wonderful and I loved it!

I didn't understand the sowing and reaping principle in those days, but that is exactly what she was doing – sowing seeds of faith into my life that built a strong foundation, and I am still standing on that today.

In the natural world we have wheat farmers, cotton farmers, and the list goes on and on. In the spiritual realm we can become faith farmers, dedicated to sowing God's seeds of faith, hope and love everywhere we go, but most importantly, into our own families! How hard is it to open your mouth and say, I love you! Every time you say it, another seed has been sown for a love crop!

PRAYER – Lord, I pray that you will help me today to generously sow seeds of love and joy and peace into the hearts of my family. I want a great harvest, so help me to sow greatly into my harvest field. Help me to dig up any wrong seeds I have sown in anger, unforgiveness or impatience, and replace them with seeds of love, forgiveness, mercy and grace. AMEN.

Teach Your Children Well

By Jeri Ingram

Whenever I am afraid, I will trust in you.
Psalm 56:3 (NKJV)

I was watching the news one night when they were interviewing a family whose home had just burned to the ground. They interviewed the little boy who was ten years old and asked how he was able to cope with this traumatic event. With maturity beyond his years he responded, "Well, I did feel afraid, but I would just say the scripture 'When I am afraid, I will trust in God', and then I would feel calm again."

I kept thinking, Wow! That boy was well-taught, and he was able to use that knowledge as an anchor for his soul in the middle of a tragedy!

In these perilous End Times in which we are now living, may we follow that wise example and make sure that our children are equipped and prepared for what lies ahead. Teach them not to focus on the trials of the present, but to keep their eyes fixed on the great glory that is to come! Talk to them about the beauty and majesty of Heaven so that it is not a strange and unfamiliar place to them. Use Bible scriptures to describe what Heaven is like so they can have a clear mental picture in their minds.

Children tend to adopt the attitude of their parents. Make it attractive and exciting to a child's mind. If you genuinely and sincerely present Heaven to them as a place of great beauty and joy, they will usually begin to feel that way about it themselves.

PRAYER – Lord, please give me creative ideas to help me strengthen and prepare my children for the perilous days ahead. Help my life to be an inspiration to my family to walk fearlessly, trusting in the great power and unfailing love of our Heavenly Father. AMEN!

The Younger The Better

By Jeri Ingram

These commandments that I give you today
are to be on your hearts. Impress them on
your children. Talk about them when you sit
at home and when you walk along the road,
when you lie down and when you get up.
Deuteronomy 6:6,7 (NIV)

My husband and I always believed that the younger our children were when they accepted Christ as their personal Savior, the more problems they could potentially be spared as they were growing up, so that was our goal from their earliest days. We looked for every opportunity to make God's love real to them. We had family devotions every night, read the Bible to them and prayed with them. We made every effort to make those times special, enjoyable and lots of fun! We wanted to make Christ attractive to them.

Our hard work and determination paid off one Sunday morning. At the time, we were still in Bible college and had gone home to Houston for the weekend, where we attended our home church. After church had ended, we saw our three-year-old daughter, Kimberly, on the platform sitting on the pastor's lap as he was praying with her to receive

Jesus. After they were done, she was so excited, she could hardly wait to tell us.

For weeks, in her little three-year-old language, she talked about it. We had a large painting of The Lord's Supper on our dining room wall, and she constantly was pointing to Jesus in the picture and saying "JeeJee"! It was obvious that the experience was very real and meaningful to her.

Two years later, we were having our family devotions one night at bedtime. Kimberly, now an articulate five-year-old, put her arms around her three-year-old sister, Kristina, and began crying. With genuine feeling, deep concern, and through tears, she began to implore Kristina to let Jesus save her from her sins!

It was adorable. She was so concerned, as though her three-year-old sister was a terrible sinner. Kristina, though, took it very seriously and began to sob. Kimberly led her in prayer as she asked to be forgiven for her sins and asked Jesus to come into her heart.

The four of us hugged, laughed, and cried with joy. It was an incredibly beautiful evening.

Now, many years later, both our girls are married and have children of their own. Those beautiful experiences from their youth are still real and meaningful. God's love is so real that even a child can understand and receive it.

PRAYER – Lord, I pray that you will give me creative ideas and inspiration to make the love of God real in my children's hearts. Help me not to miss any opportunities, as my time with them is short before they go out into the world on their own. I pray that you will help me to prepare them for whatever lies ahead, and that nothing will keep them from fulfilling their destiny. AMEN

Dancing On Streets Of Gold

By Jeri Ingram

Delight yourself also in the Lord and He shall
give you the desires of your heart. Psalm 37:4
(NKJV)

Both my parents, Tinky and Gerald, died within the same
month. Dad was buried one Saturday, and mom was buried
the next Saturday. Instead of that being a tragic situation,
our family thought it was incredibly beautiful! They had
been married for sixty-one years, and they had always said
they wanted to go to Heaven together, and we believe God
honored their wishes.

When my husband was speaking at my mom's funeral, he
made the statement, "Tinky and Gerald had a rendezvous
in heaven, and now they are dancing on streets of gold." We
wept tears of joy as we visualized it.

During the funerals, different family members shared stories
of how my parents' marriage had impacted them. We learned
later that one young couple had an appointment scheduled at
the divorce court, but they were so inspired after hearing my
parents' stories, they cancelled it and renewed their wedding
vows instead!

A few days after the funerals were over, my sister came across a Bible that dad had given to our mother on their 55th anniversary. Inside the cover he had written a note to my mother that said, "Let's go together, hon. Love, Gerald."

Little did he know that God would grant him the desire of his heart. Their marriage not only left a strong legacy for our family but inspired others as well.

When we endeavor to live our lives following God's biblical pattern, He uses our lives to touch others, even when we're unaware.

PRAYER – Lord, help my marriage to be an inspiration to others in a time when marriages are under great satanic onslaught. Help me to always be mindful of the sacredness of the covenant we made when we said "I do", and let our faithfulness to that covenant be an encouragement to other couples to stay faithful in the middle of their strongest battles. AMEN

Divorce, $49.95

By Jeri Ingram

What therefore God has joined together, let
not man put asunder. Mark 10:9 (KJV)

We were pastoring a church in our hometown of Pasadena, Texas, when one day as I was driving to the church, I noticed a new sign that had been placed on top of one of the buildings I passed every day. In big, bold letters it read, *DIVORCE, $49.95!*

I was speechless! I kept thinking, "Is this what marriage has come to in America – something to be ended easily – quick and cheap!?"

Some years later after we moved to New England to pastor, there was a young couple getting married in our church. The bride was a lovely Jewish girl, born in America, and the groom was a handsome Nigerian man studying to be a doctor.

The groom asked my husband to call his father in Nigeria, who was worried about the marriage. The groom was in his mid-30's and old enough to make decisions for himself, but my husband appreciated the respect the groom showed for his father and agreed to call him.

After my husband and the father shared greetings on the phone, the father began to explain his deep concerns. He said, "I'm afraid for my son to marry an American girl because everyone in America gets divorced. We value marriage here in Nigeria."

My husband was heartbroken and told him that America had not always been that way and asked him to pray for our country. He told him that, while it is true that many do divorce, there are also many who do not, and while there are no guarantees, if the bride and groom would follow Biblical instructions, they could have a successful marriage.

That is God's desire for all of us – to simply follow his instructions. Then *DIVORCE, $49.95 stores* would no longer be needed.

The couple moved away, but the last we heard from them, they had been married approximately ten years and were still going strong! God is good!

PRAYER – Lord, I pray for every marriage in America. I pray that you would strengthen the bond between every husband and wife and help them begin to view each other with the respect and love that you intended for married couples to have. Let the wind of your precious Holy Spirit blow through every home renewing and reviving the sacredness of the marriage vows, to the honor and glory of your holy name. AMEN

Her Dying Wish

By Jeri Ingram

Every good gift and every perfect gift is
from above, and cometh down from the
Father of lights. James 1 :17 (KJV)

The first church we ever pastored was in Rhode Island.
Sister Perry was an elderly widow who had been a long-time
member of the church. She was a devout Christian, and she
never, ever missed church services.

Our family sort of adopted her and took her with us
whenever we attended church picnics or other outings. She
was always a pleasure to have around.

Years later, after we had resigned and moved back to our
home town in Texas to pastor a church there, we got word
that Sister Perry had passed away. The surprising thing was
that she had passed away while sitting in church during a
Sunday morning service.

Later, we learned from some of her family members that
she loved attending church so much that her prayer for
many years had been to pass away while sitting in a service.
Imagine that!

How wonderful to know the God we serve loves us so much that the desires of our heart are important to him, and his generosity to us is beyond anything we could ever imagine.

PRAYER – Lord, what a joy it is to know that the God who does such great and magnificent things like the creation of the world, or salvation of our souls, also cares about every little thing in our lives. I thank you for your love and care for your children. AMEN

There Is No Marriage In Heaven!

By Jeri Ingram

For when the dead rise, they will neither
marry nor be given in marriage. In this
respect they will be like the angels in Heaven.
Mark 12:25 (NLT)

Through the years I have heard people say they don't understand why there is no marriage in Heaven. The thought made them sad.

Being happily married for fifty-six years, I can certainly relate to that. I can't imagine living in heaven and not being married to my husband after all these years of being together here on earth.

When I was a brand-new Christian, I had an unusual experience with the Lord that perhaps gave me a glimmer of understanding. It was Sunday morning, and I was in church. We were in the middle of a powerful worship service that was so powerful it felt like there were angels in the room.

As we were worshipping, the level of intensity began to swell and grow. The presence of Almighty God became so strong I felt I would explode with joy! My hands were lifted high in the air, and I was singing with strength and gusto I didn't know was possible.

Suddenly, as I was singing and looking upwards, I saw Jesus! He was suspended in the rafters with his long white robes flowing down and his outstretched arms were reaching towards me. I couldn't see his face, but I could see his distinct outline through a brilliant white glow.

My eyes were fixed on him as I reached my hands out towards him, and I began to have the sensation of lifting into the air. I understood what Paul was saying when he said he couldn't tell if he was in the body or out. I felt like I was going up and up – higher and higher – and the level of sheer ecstasy was beyond anything I had ever experienced in my life. I didn't want it to end.

Then gradually the vision began to fade and I drifted back to my seat in the sanctuary. I felt sad that it was over.

Through the years, whenever I have thought of that experience, I have found myself wondering if perhaps that is why we will not miss the existence of marriage in Heaven. No earthly relationship could ever compare to the rich intimacy and sheer ecstasy we will enjoy in God's presence in heaven. Truly, it will be joy unspeakable and full of glory!

PRAYER – Lord, how grateful we are to serve a mighty, powerful, wonderful, generous, loving God like you! If you never did another thing for us, giving us assurance of eternity in Heaven with you is beyond our ability to express our gratitude in words. We thank you, and we look forward to that day when we step into your glorious presence! We bless your Holy Name!!!! AMEN

The Power Of Communion

By Jeri Ingram

> While they were eating, Jesus took bread,
> and when he had given thanks, he broke it
> and gave it to his disciples, saying, "Take and
> eat; this is my body". Then he took a cup
> and when he had given thanks, he gave it to
> them, saying, "Drink from it, all of you. This
> is my blood of the covenant, which is poured
> out for many for the forgiveness of sins.
> Matthew 26: 26-28 (NIV)

One of the most painful illnesses I have ever experienced was shingles. It hurt when I sat down, laid down, stood up, walked or stood still. In other words, it hurt constantly, no matter what position I was in. It had been going on for a couple of weeks without any relief.

I decided to increase my time with the Lord each day. I knew the Bible said that he who seeks the Lord will find Him, so I set out on that quest. I decided to take communion each day with my devotion time. It was a beautiful time of worship and meditating on the love of God.

One day, sitting in my dining room taking communion alone, I became so enveloped in His presence that I began to worship Him. I worshipped and praised till I felt lost in

His presence. The tears of love poured down my face and joy filled my heart till I thought it would burst.

When my worship time ended and I got up to go into the other room, I walked down the hallway and suddenly became aware of something --- the pain was gone!

Before I had taken communion, the pain from the shingles had been very intense. During my time of communion and worship, the Lord had reached down and touched me and I was completely and totally healed!

The healing power of God is released when we take communion with faith and love in our hearts.

PRAYER – Lord, you willingly allowed yourself to be beaten and crucified so that we could be healed and saved. Then you instructed us to continually take communion as a reminder of the incredible sacrifice you paid for us. We can never thank you enough. You are a wonderful Savior and we bless your Holy Name! AMEN

Don't Be Anxious

By Jeri Ingram

Even though Jesus was God's son, he learned
obedience from the things he suffered.
Hebrews 5:8 (NLT)

It had been a difficult year – one filled with stress. Normally, I am a pretty positive person, but that year I found myself continually giving in to the stress that surrounded our circumstances. The strange thing was that every time I gave in to the stress, I felt a big lump form right in the middle of my chest. Each time it happened, the lump felt larger, causing more pressure.

That went on for a few months and I finally became deathly ill. My husband took me to the emergency room, and as the professional medical people performed their tests, I laid on the table feeling weaker than I had ever felt in my life. In fact, I felt like I could have easily slipped out of this world into eternity.

Finally, the doctor came in and said, "You have an infection in the area of your windpipe." I had never heard of anything like that. He pointed to the area of the infection, and it was the exact spot where I had been experiencing the lump in the middle of my chest. I knew the prolonged stress and anxiety I had been harboring had caused the illness.

That experience is actually one of the best things that ever happened to me, because even though it happened many years ago, it is still very vivid in my mind. Every time I am tempted to give in to worry, stress, or anxiety, I immediately remember that bad experience and am compelled to push worry away and start releasing my faith.

God continually tells us to be not afraid and have no anxiety. It's about time we learned to just simply TRUST HIM!

PRAYER – Lord, help me today to keep my thoughts focused on you and your great love and care for your children. When anxiety tries to raise its ugly head, give me the grace and strength to push it away. No matter how bad circumstances seem, your power is always greater! I CHOOSE to trust you!!! AMEN

Laughter Brings Healing

By Jeri Ingram

A merry heart doeth good like a medicine.
Proverbs 17:22 (KJV)

I had been terribly sick for a couple of weeks with an infection in my windpipe. I was still in bed and feeling very weak. The sad thing was that our oldest daughter, Kimberly, was being crowned Homecoming Princess of the 7th grade that night, and I was too sick to go. My family all felt bad about leaving me, but I insisted they go and support Kimberly on her special night.

Reluctantly, they all left, and, honestly, I felt a little depressed. The house was too quiet, and I felt so alone! After a while, though, in the middle of my pity party, I heard the still, small voice of the Lord saying something that surprised me. He said, "You know, a merry heart is like a medicine. Why don't you laugh a little?"

My goodness! I was too weak to move, much less laugh! But at the Lord's instruction, I was determined to try, so I mustered up the strength to force out a small giggle. It was hard, but I felt a small surge of energy flow through me, so I forced out another giggle and experienced another little burst of energy. So, I continued giggling, then resting, giggling, then resting, over and over until I had enough energy to actually laugh!

After a while, I felt enough strength to get off the couch. I began walking through every room of the house and laughing in every room. The more I laughed, the stronger I felt. By the time I got through the last room, I felt strong. I mean, I felt as normal as if I had never been sick at all. I was healed!

I immediately thought of Peter's mother-in-law and how she had been sick with a fever, but when she was prayed for, she was instantly healed and got up and cooked them all a meal as though she had never been ill. I spent the rest of the evening rejoicing and thanking God!

Later that evening, when everyone arrived home, I met them at the door, completely well and whole, and still laughing! The look of surprise on their faces was priceless. God has a wonderful sense of humor!

The next time you are sick, begin to praise and worship God; even begin to laugh. Let the joy of the Lord flow through you. Watch how the love of God flows through your life, bringing healing, wholeness and joy.

PRAYER – Lord, I love you! What a joy it is to serve you! Even when my circumstances are difficult, I can still rejoice to know that I do not have to face it alone. You are always with me and you will never leave me! I rejoice in your great love for me, Lord, no matter what, and I bless your Holy Name! AMEN

The Daughter Of Satan

By Jeri Ingram

He that wins souls is wise.
Proverbs 11:30 (KJV)

While my husband was attending Bible college, we were part of a jail ministry that went to the local jail every Sunday afternoon. My husband would go with the men to minister to the male prisoners, while I would go with the women to visit the female prisoners.

One Sunday afternoon, two ladies and I went to visit a new inmate named Gigi. The guards had warned us to be careful around her as she was considered dangerous. At gunpoint, she had marched her husband out under a streetlight one night and shot him through the head. She had a big, bold tattoo on her arm that read, *Daughter of Satan.*

So, the two ladies and I prayed together, then went to her cell door to talk to her through the bars. She had a wooden door for privacy inside the cell door, and when she heard our voices she screamed in a shrill voice, "I HATE WOMEN PREACHERS!" Then she slammed the wooden door in our faces ... HARD!

We quickly scurried away so we could regroup and figure out a plan. I'm not sure how it happened, but somehow the two ladies decided I should go back to her cell --- alone!

I felt it was important to try to reach her, so I agreed to their plan. I made my way back to her cell, and when Gigi learned I was the only woman there, she opened the wooden door, possibly not feeling so intimidated. We had a chat that went surprisingly well, and I promised to see her again. Each Sunday afternoon I went back to see her, and she was obviously softening.

About three months later, I was sharing with Gigi how much Jesus loved her, and her tears began to flow. Her hands slowly slid down the bars as she fell to her knees. I joined her on my knees on the other side of the bars, and she tearfully repented and asked Jesus into her heart.

What an incredible moment! I felt like I could almost hear the heavenly host of angels singing and rejoicing in heaven. Gigi had come home to Jesus! There is truly nothing that can compare with the joy of leading the lost to Christ!

PRAYER -- Lord, please lead me to someone today who is hungry to know you. Give me boldness, courage and the right words to minister your love and grace to them. Help me to lead them to wonderful salvation through our Lord, Jesus Christ. AMEN

We Have Power Over The Enemy

By Jeri Ingram

Resist the devil and he will flee from you.
James 4:7 (NIV)

After Gigi, an inmate at the local jail, gave her heart to the Lord, we learned that she was to be transferred to the state prison for women in Huntsville, Texas. We felt it was important for her to have a Christian baptism before she left, so our group leader asked the sheriff for permission to take her to a local church service where she could be baptized. We were all so excited when the sheriff not only agreed to escort her to the church, but he and his wife even took her shopping for a dress for the occasion.

That was a glorious night as Gigi testified of what God had done for her. Then she tearfully shared that she felt God was sending her to the Huntsville prison as a missionary, and asked us to pray for her that she would accomplish all that God wanted her to do there. Tears flowed all over the church building that night!

After Gigi was moved to Huntsville, I missed my weekly visits with her, and I wondered how she was doing. The prison was several hours from where we lived, so my husband and I determined to try to make the trip to visit her as often as we could.

The first couple of visits went fine, but the third time we went, we learned there was a new warden with new rules, and I was no longer allowed to go in with my husband to visit her.

Disappointed, I went to sit in the waiting room. I began to pray because, quite honestly, there was a very dark and bad feeling that had not been there the first couple of visits. I sat there, silently praying in tongues for a breakthrough, but the atmosphere seemed so dark and intense I felt like I could hardly breathe. I just kept on praying!

As I sat with my head slightly tilted upwards, I suddenly saw the most chilling sight I had ever seen. I had seen a few visions before, but nothing like this. Overhead in the rafters was a large ring of demons circling the room. They were black and looked similar to bats. Their wings were outstretched and were interlocked together forming a tight, unbreakable circle. I knew the Lord was showing me what was causing the terrible feeling in the building, and I knew I had to resist their evil power through prayer until it was broken, so I kept on praying!

After a period of time, something happened! The circle of demons seemed to be knocked backwards, forcing two of the demons' bat-like wings to come apart. Once that happened, the whole circle began to fall apart. Once the circle fell apart, all the demons began to flee out of the building, and the vision ended.

About half an hour later, my husband returned from his visit and shared how the first part of his visit had been unsuccessful. Gigi seemed tense and bound and could barely talk. Dick said he also felt bound and could barely speak. He said the atmosphere was dark and oppressive, but then something unexplainable happened.

Suddenly, the dark, oppressive, heavy atmosphere lifted and was gone, instantly replaced with a clear, light, free and pleasant atmosphere. He said Gigi's whole countenance changed, and she began to joyfully share different ways that God was helping her and even using her to minister to some of her cellmates.

After I shared with my husband what I had experienced in the waiting room, we both knew exactly what had happened. By continually praying, the power of God had been released to fight against demonic forces in the building. I resisted the devil, and he fled – exactly as God promises in his Holy Word!

This same God-given power and authority is available to all Christians – you just must believe!

PRAYER – Father, your Word has made us aware of the demonic forces at work in this world. But your Word has also shown us that we have the supernatural power of Christ within us to defeat those evil forces. Today, by your grace, I take authority over all demonic forces that would come against me or my family, and I thank you for your overcoming victory! AMEN

You Must Take The Land!

By Jeri Ingram

> I have given you this land. Go in and take
> possession of the land the Lord swore He
> would give to you. Deuteronomy 1:8 (NIV)

My husband and I both felt the Lord was calling us to move to New England to pioneer a church there. We began to pray that all our needs for the move would be met -- including the right home to live in.

One Sunday night during church we were sitting side by side on the platform and the presence of the Lord was especially real and powerful that evening. As I prayed, the face of a woman I knew in the church came before me. I began to weep as I heard the still, small voice of God say, "Give her your grandfather clock."

My grandfather clock! It was my most prized possession that was a gift from my husband on our anniversary. The Lord continued, however, impressing upon me to plant it as a seed for the home we would need in New England.

I leaned over and whispered to my husband what had happened and asked him if it was ok with him to give the clock away. He chuckled, raised his eyebrows, and said, "Yes, I just made the last payment on it!"

So, that night we agreed in prayer that we would give it as a seed for our new home in New England. When we delivered the clock to the woman, she was thrilled and blown away because she had been in our home and had seen the clock, and had always admired it.

After arriving in New England, friends directed us to a house that had just come open on the market. It was almost brand new and had been professionally decorated. It was more beautiful than anything I had ever expected, and even though we didn't know what our income would be at our new church, as soon as we walked in the front door, we had the strong sense that this was supposed to be our home. We immediately made an appointment to meet with the owner, an attorney from New York City.

The very next day, he met us at the house, along with our two daughters. His name was Bruno, and he fit the exact stereotype I imagined for a New York lawyer. He was a big man with a gravelly, gruff voice. He asked all kind of questions about the church we would be pastoring, and decided the purchase was too great a financial risk for us. He politely turned us down and left.

It could have ended right there, and we could have given up, but we had planted a good seed into good soil in obedience to the word from God, and we felt in our hearts that this was the house God intended for us, so we decided to stand in faith and believe God!

After the attorney left, the four of us sat in the car in the driveway and began to pray. We knew in our hearts the Lord had told us to plant the grandfather clock as a seed for our home, so we asked the Lord if this truly was the home God intended us to have that he would please keep Bruno awake all night and unable to sleep until he agreed to sell to us. We prayed and agreed together, confident that God had heard our prayer.

The next morning at 8:00 a.m. our phone rang. It was the unmistakable voice of Bruno. He growled into the phone, "I don't know why, but I couldn't sleep all night! I kept thinking about your family having that home and I decided to let you have it so I can get some rest!"

We thanked him, hung up and praised God! We moved in shortly after that, and it was a wonderful home for us as long as we lived in that town. We never had any financial problem with it.

Sometimes you can have total faith for something, even have a direct word from God concerning that very matter, but it still doesn't happen automatically. Sometimes you must go a step further and TAKE THE LAND!

PRAYER – Lord, there are things I have been believing for. Would you reveal to me if there is something I need to do in order to take that land? My desire is to trust and believe you in every area of my life, and I thank you for your grace and help. AMEN

God Understands What You're Going Through

By Jeri Ingram

Everyone who has left houses or brothers or
sisters or father or mother or wife or children
or fields for my sake will receive a hundred
times as much and will inherit eternal life.
Matthew 19:29 (NIV)

God called us to pioneer a church in New England. It was
a big move for us. My husband and I were both born in
Houston, Texas, and had lived in Texas all our lives. In
our minds, New England was so far away that it almost
seemed as if we were moving to a foreign country. We
were designated as home missionaries by our denomination,
which meant we would have to itinerate and raise financial
support before making the move. We decided it would be
best to sell or give away everything except our clothes,
dishes and linens.

There was only one item that was hard for me to part
with. Our daughters had a brand-new, peppermint-candy-
striped swing set that their grandparents had recently given
them. We sold it to a young man with two little boys, and
I remember the day he came in his pickup truck along with
his sons to pick it up. As they drove off with the swing set

in the back of their truck, I stood there watching them drive away and sadly picturing our girls joyfully swinging on the swings. I was heartbroken, and tears started running down my cheeks. Then I heard the tender voice of God say to me, "I know how you feel. I felt that way when my Son lost his life."

My tears instantly dried up! I realized that anything we lose in this life is nothing in comparison to what God gave up for us! Anything we can do in this life for him should be considered a privilege and an honor. He gave his life freely so that we can have eternal life. We could never outgive his extreme generosity!

PRAYER – Lord, I thank you with all my heart for the great sacrifice you made by giving up your Son so that we could have eternal life in heaven with you. I know we will never fully understand what a price it was for you, but it is with joy and gratitude that we spend our lives in service to you, our Heavenly Father. AMEN

Thank God For Dr. Gus!

By Jeri Ingram

Listen to advice and accept discipline, and at
the end you will be counted among the wise.
Proverbs19:20 (NIV)

When our first daughter, Kimberly, was born, we were like many first-time parents about raising their babies -- clueless! Oh, we knew how to feed her and change her diapers, and we certainly knew how to love her and play with her, but if anything serious happened that was not addressed in the baby books we were constantly referring to, we didn't know what to do.

When she was around a year old, she was the cutest baby you ever saw -- sparkly, bubbly and so much fun that people were always asking to babysit her. But she was not a good sleeper from the time she was born, and bedtime became a challenge. We tried everything, including putting her into a stroller and taking turns walking her through the house for hours to try and coax her to sleep.

BIG MISTAKE! She loved it! In fact, she loved it so much that she would keep herself awake until very late before finally giving in to sleep. We were exhausted, and out of ideas!

At that time, my husband was working for the Houston Police Department. One morning, after a long and arduous night of strolling, he dressed in his usual police uniform and left for work. On his way, he decided to drop by our pediatrician's office on the way to work to get some advice. Dr. Gus was a wonderful doctor with an abundance of common sense who seemed to instinctively know what to do in just about any given situation involving children.

When my husband walked into the doctor's office in his police uniform asking to see Dr. Gus, it scared the receptionist and she immediately ushered him in ahead of everyone in the waiting room. Dr. Gus listened as my husband explained our problem, and when finished, he shocked my husband with his response!

Usually, a very patient and good-natured man, Dr. Gus looked my husband in the eye and sternly said, "Who is in charge of your home? Is it you or your baby? You go home tonight, you kiss and hug that baby and assure her everything is alright, then you put that baby in her bed, then leave and close the door -- and don't you open that door again till the next morning!"

My husband left Dr. Gus' office in shock and embarrassment, but we did exactly what he ordered us to do. It was hard! We stood in the middle of the living room floor most of the night listening to her scream, with me sobbing and Dick holding me in his arms reassuring me she was ok. Finally, early the next morning she fell asleep. We had to repeat the process the next night as well, but it didn't take as long before she fell asleep. After two nights, we never had to do it again.

Thank God for Dr. Gus who had the wisdom and courage to help us onto the right track. And thank God that my husband took his role as head of our household seriously and didn't allow pride to prevent him from asking for much-needed advice. Our home became so much more peaceful after that! We followed biblical instructions about seeking advice, and it worked. It is amazing how instructions from God's Word can help us in any situation.

PRAYER – Lord, I pray that pride will not stop me from seeking advice and wisdom from others when it is needed. Help me to keep my heart and mind open to your instruction, directions and even correction in my life. I am relying on you to keep my feet on the straight and narrow path, so that one day I may hear the lovely words, "Well done, thou good & faithful servant." Matthew 25:21 (KJV) AMEN

You Must Be Born Again!

By Jeri Ingram

> You should not be surprised at my saying you
> must be born again. John 3:7 (NIV)

My husband and I were both raised in church. We attended Sunday School, we sang in the choir, we attended the Youth Fellowship as teenagers, and when we were old enough, we became Sunday School teachers. We were faithful church members, but there was a problem – while we were very religious, we had no idea about being born again.

Growing up in the church, we were proud of being good Christians; however, there was an unexplainable hunger in my heart. I would walk through my house thinking, "Is this all there is to life? You get up, you get dressed, you go through the day, you get undressed, you go to bed, and the next day you do the same thing again, day after day after day." I did not realize at the time that it was God himself placing those thoughts in my mind, causing me to think about life in a deeper way, creating a hunger in my heart for God.

One day my sister, Maggie, came home from a Christian retreat she had attended over the weekend. She said she had become born-again. We had never heard the term, but we were intrigued and began asking questions.

I called the church office and asked if they could explain what the term born-again meant. They blew me off, and it was obvious they had no clue what it meant either. So, I picked up my phone book and called other churches in the area and asked the same question. No one knew, and there were some that actually hung up on me! I was mystified. I thought, shouldn't churches be willing and prepared to answer spiritual questions of people seeking answers?

Soon after that, my sister gave us a book called "The Cross & the Switchblade" by David Wilkerson. I read it and looked up every scripture in the Bible it referred to, just to verify it. When I was through, I understood how to be born-again and also how to be baptized in the Holy Spirit. Oh, my gosh! Was I ever excited! I found answers to all my questions.

My sister shared with us about her born-again experience at the Christian retreat, and I knew for sure that was what I wanted. We prayed together and I asked Jesus to come into my heart and forgive me of all my sins. I was born again and finally understood that Christianity is not about religion, but instead, it is a relationship with Christ!!!

Pretty soon, someone told me about a ladies' prayer meeting where I could go for prayer to be baptized in the Holy Spirit. I couldn't wait! I've never been so excited about anything in my life! When I walked into the house with all the ladies on that Saturday morning, I just dropped my purse on the floor and blurted out, "I'm here for the baptism in the Holy Spirit."

Everyone immediately stopped what they were doing and surrounded me. They excitedly laid their hands on my shoulders and head and began praying for me. Tears began pouring down my face as I lifted my hands high in the air in total surrender to the Lord. I don't know how long we had been praying when I began speaking in tongues, but the moment it happened, the ladies surprisingly began squealing, and jerking their hands off of me, and jumping away from me. Later, they said they felt electrical shocks coming from me when I began speaking in tongues.

Wow! I had become born-again the week before, and now I was baptized in the Holy Spirit! From that day, my life changed totally, and I have never been the same! It is now over half a century since that day in 1969, and the change that happened to me then is as strong and powerful today as it was then.

TO GOD BE ALL THE GLORY!!!!!!!

PRAYER – Lord, I pray that you will help me walk in the power of the Holy Spirit that you promised in the Book of Acts. I've never experienced anything so wonderful in all of my life and I'm asking you for the ability to share this marvelous gift with others. Please open doors for me to talk to people who are hungry, and give me the power and the right words to share with them. Thank you for supernatural enabling through your Holy Spirit. AMEN

Our First Miracle!

By Jeri Ingram

He was wounded for our transgressions;
he was bruised for our iniquities; the
chastisement of our peace was upon
Him; and with his stripes we are healed.
Isaiah 53:5 (KJV)

My husband and I both grew up in the same denominational church. We knew about God, but we didn't have a personal relationship with him. God, however, sometimes uses unusual situations to draw people to him, & that's what he did in our case.

When our first daughter was born, it was no time before she began experiencing symptoms of severe allergies. After doing all the standard allergy tests when she was six months old, her pediatrician told us, "Your daughter is allergic to only two things -- FOOD & AIR!" He was so right! Everything she ate made her sick. Playing outdoors made her sick. She was always getting sick, running fever, throwing up, diarrhea, etc. and we were at our wits end.

By the time she was eighteen months old, we were desperate and searching for answers. Our search led us to God's promises for divine healing in the Bible. The medical profession was unable to help her, so one evening, when she was very ill with a high fever, we took her to a Pentecostal church to be prayed for. After returning home, I knew beyond all doubt that God had touched her.

I'm not one to put deadlines on a Sovereign God, but somehow, I knew deep in my heart that he intended her healing to take place that night, so I set my faith to see it manifest by midnight. We laid her on the couch where we could keep an eye on her. She was so weak and her fever so high that she was not moving at all. We began to pray. We thanked God for her healing, even before it manifested.

We were watching the clock with anticipation, and at the exact stroke of midnight, she sat straight up on the couch and broke into an intense sweat. She continued sweating until her fever was totally gone! She got up and started playing, as though she had never been sick at all!

The next morning, I felt as though God wanted me to demonstrate my faith by feeding her the worst foods of her allergies – toast with butter, cereal with milk, and orange juice. Any one of those foods would have made her terribly sick previously, but she had no reaction at all. She was healed!

That was many years ago, and she's now grown and married with three beautiful children. She has never had an allergy since that day.

We give God honor and glory and great praise! That healing blessed our daughter with good health, and also was the motivating force that God used to bring us to salvation. Who wouldn't want to serve a God like that!!!!!!

PRAYER – Lord, I believe in your healing power. It was provided for by the stripes you received on your back at Calvary. Today, help me to receive all you provided for me and share with others the miraculous work that was accomplished at the Cross. AMEN

Salvation For My Husband

By Jeri Ingram

They replied, "Believe in the Lord Jesus and
you will be saved – you and your household".
Acts 16:31 (NIV)

I don't want to share the full story of my husband's salvation
because that is his story to tell, but there are a few things
that happened from my perspective that I believe are worth
mentioning.

During the time of our spiritual awakening, my sister,
Maggie, was single and living with us. Our oldest daughter,
Kimberly, was just a baby and went to bed early every
night. My husband, Dick, was working the night shift for
the Houston Police Department, so that meant my sister
and I, who had both just become born-again, Spirit-filled
believers, had several hours each evening we could devote to
prayer and Bible reading. It was wonderful! We would light
candles in the living room for ambience and begin praying!
It was a very powerful time!

Of course, we spent a lot of time praying for Dick's heart to
be opened to receive the great blessings God was offering to
us! I was constantly praying and leaving tracts laying around
the house, anything I could think of that might be of interest

to him. It occurred to me that, as a police officer, the book "The Cross & the Switchblade" by David Wilkerson might appeal to him. So, one night before I went to bed, I left it on the coffee table in the living room.

As it turned out, that very night he was having an unusual encounter with God that made him totally open and ready to receive from the Lord, so when he came in from work and saw the book, he just threw off his gun and hat and sat down on the couch and began reading. He made it halfway through before going to bed.

The next night, he finished the book. He was so moved, he got onto his knees in front of our living room couch and asked Jesus to forgive his sins and come into his heart. He also asked to be baptized in the Holy Spirit, and the next thing he knew, he was speaking in a heavenly language.

The next morning, he couldn't wait to tell us what had happened. He had truly been born-again, and he said the unusually beautiful heavenly language God gave him sounded very much like the language of the Choctaw Indians he remembered as a boy when visiting his grandfather in Oklahoma. Our home was filled with joy and excitement that day. We could not stop thanking and praising God!!

Before all this happened, our lives had been kind of average and even boring at times. But when we came to know and love the Lord, there was no more monotony. He filled our lives with joy and excitement, and our lives have truly never been the same!

PRAYER – Lord, I thank you for the priceless gift of salvation for me, my husband, and my entire family. Give me the grace to share with others this great message that they too may enjoy the gift of eternal life. AMEN

Standing On The Word Of God!

By Jeri Ingram

He sent His Word and healed them …
Psalm 107:20a (NIV)

We were living in Waxahachie, Texas, where my husband was attending Southwestern Assemblies of God University. Our oldest daughter, Kimberly, was three, and our youngest daughter, Kristina, was a baby. Kristina caught a very bad cold that she couldn't seem to shake. No matter what we did to help her, she just kept getting worse and worse. We took her to the doctor and faithfully gave her medicine, but her fever soared. We prayed and prayed, but there was no change! It was a very scary time, and my husband and I took turns sitting by her bed trying to keep her fever down.

One day I had just had it! It seemed as though the life was being sucked out of our baby and I had to do something. I went through our home looking for Bibles and gathered a whole stack of them. I opened every Bible to a different scripture on healing, highlighted the scriptures in yellow, and placed the Bibles in strategic locations in every room in the house, with the Bibles laying open at the highlighted page. Every time I walked by a Bible, I stopped and read the highlighted scripture *OUT LOUD*! I wanted the devil to hear me. I also knew the Bible says, "Faith cometh by *HEARING*, and hearing by the Word of God" (Romans 10:17 KJV), so I knew the more I read the scriptures *OUT LOUD,* my faith would be strengthened.

This went on for two or three days with absolutely no improvement, but one morning we walked into her room and there she was, sitting up and playing! Her fever was gone, as though she had never been sick. There was no gradual improvement like you would normally see. She just went from being very, very sick, to being totally well. Only God can do that. I knew in my heart that the scriptures we had been reading over her day and night had released healing power into her body.

Once again, as we stood in faith on his Word, he fulfilled his promises! What a wonderful God we serve!!!!

PRAYER – Lord, I pray for my children today that you will keep them well and whole and free from sin, sickness and harm. You are a wonderful Heavenly Father who faithfully cares for his children. I trust you! AMEN

The Gift Of Hospitality

By Jeri Ingram

Share with the Lord's people who are in need.
Practice hospitality. Romans 12:13

My husband and I both grew up in the south where hospitality was an important part of our culture, and we have seen firsthand that it truly makes life more enjoyable. Over the next few stories, I will share some experiences involving this wonderful gift.

According to the dictionary, hospitality means "the friendly and generous reception and entertainment of guests, visitors, or strangers."

While growing up, we saw our parents demonstrate hospitality in our homes, and it was from them we learned the beauty of it. When we were married and had our own home, we tried to carry on that tradition. For example, we would do simple things for guests who stayed overnight, like placing a tray at their bedside with bottles of water and snacks – any little thing we could think of to make their stay in our home more comfortable.

One time an elderly missionary stayed with us. We explained to our girls that we were all to show great honor to this missionary for her long and faithful years on the mission field. Our daughters took that very seriously.

When she arrived at our home that evening, our nine-year-old Kimberly took the woman by the hand and led her to the room we had prepared for her. We had not given the girls any specific instructions, other than to be polite and courteous, so I was surprised when Kimberly had her sit down on the bed while reaching down to remove her shoes and make her comfortable. She then brought her a hot cup of tea, and the missionary was moved to tears. She said she did not know when she had been treated with such kindness.

Now our daughters are grown, and both graciously practice the art of hospitality. Our youngest daughter, Kristina, is over the Hospitality Ministry at the church and is also a talented decorator. She creates incredibly beautiful events for large numbers of people, and her events are always memorable.

While pastoring, my husband served as Presbyter, and we regularly hosted events for the ministers of our Section. He always trusted Kristina to add her touch and make those events beautiful. Pastors do not have easy lives, and he wanted them to be ministered to with beautiful and caring hospitality. Over and over the people attending would comment, "We feel so refreshed after attending Kristina's events. Her hard work and care shines through!"

That is what the gift of hospitality is supposed to do – remind people how much God loves and cares for them!

PRAYER – Lord, these are difficult and challenging times in which we are living. Show us creative ways to use the gift of hospitality to refresh and renew people who are weary and tired in the battle. Help us use this beautiful gift to remind people of your love and care for them, no matter what is going on in their lives. AMEN

The Importance Of Hospitality

By Jeri Ingram

Dear friend, when you extend hospitality
to Christian brothers and sisters, even when
they are strangers, you make the faith visible.
3 John 1:5 (MSG)

As pastors, we always tried to teach and emphasize to our church members how important it was for us to demonstrate hospitality to reach our community for the Lord.

After 9/11, the heaviness of that horrific event was on everyone's mind. It was during that time that the Lord began to impress upon us the extreme importance and necessity of hospitality. The thought kept going through my mind that the Lord wants to release something into the Body of Christ that is going to help people get through the perilous End Times --- the Gift of Hospitality. And shortly after that, we began having experiences that revealed to us what he meant.

The first event was when a dynamic young pastor in his thirties from North Carolina stayed in our home for a week. We felt the Lord wanted us to show him love and encourage him, so we rearranged our busy schedule to spend time with him.

We listened intently as he talked. We then shared some of our experiences with him, and he had many questions, which we took the time needed to carefully answer. It was a joy to see someone so young with such hunger and passion for God, and we told him so.

Soon after he left, we received a call from him. He said he had been very discouraged in the ministry before he came to visit us. While with us, he said the love and hospitality we showed him in our home so refreshed and revitalized him that he was eager to get back to ministry again.

The Gift of Hospitality revived this young man in his service to the Lord!

PRAYER – Lord, lead me to people who are weary in the battle and just need some refreshing. Then show me how to demonstrate your love to them in ways in which they can receive and be blessed. Thank you for this wonderful gift you provided for our benefit. AMEN

The Gift Of Hospitality
Brings Refreshing

by Jeri Ingram

It is good work you are doing, helping these
travelers on their way, showing hospitality
worthy of God Himself. 3 John 1:6 (MSG)

Another time we had some missionaries from a very remote country stay in our home. We lived just south of Boston, and their son needed some medical treatment in Boston, so they asked if they could stay with us. They had been missionaries for years in very difficult places, and had even ministered to leper colonies, as well as abandoned children left on the streets to die.

Once again, we felt the Lord telling us to refresh these veteran missionaries through the gift of hospitality, so we made sure their room was beautifully decorated with flowers and a nice tray beside their bed with nuts, M&M's, small bottles of water and some magazines.

We kept beautiful music playing to create a peaceful atmosphere and served them a nice breakfast each morning. We made sure to take plenty of time to fellowship with them, as we felt they probably didn't get too much Christian fellowship in the remote country where they lived and ministered.

As they were leaving, they kept saying over and over they had not felt so refreshed in years, and felt strengthened to go back to their country and continue the work there.

We saw the Gift of Hospitality at work, bringing healing and much needed refreshing. This is how God wants us to minister to one another as the perilous end times become more and more difficult.

PRAYER – Lord, we know you want us to minister to one another, and even more so as the times become more perilous and difficult. Bring people to us that we can help and comfort as they travel through life. Help us do for them as we would want others to do for us. AMEN

The Gift Of Hospitality
Is A Strong Weapon

By Jeri Ingram

These believers deserve any help we can give
them. In providing meals & a bed, we become
their companions in spreading the truth.
3 John 1:7 (MSG)

We had another experience that made us see that the Gift
of Hospitality can not only be used to minister healing and
refreshing to God's people, but it can also be used to tear
down strongholds of Satan as well.

A friend of ours, who is a missionary evangelist, started an
incredible ministry in Russia when the Communist Wall
came down. Their fledgling ministry was exploding over
there, but they could not find any suitable office space,
which was desperately needed. They prayed, they fasted, but
they said it was like there was a wall or a stronghold they
simply couldn't find a way to break through.

Finally, the missionary evangelist came back to the States,
and while here, he visited our church to minister one
Sunday evening. After he preached, my husband took up a
nice offering for him, and the missionary was thrilled!

But my husband wasn't done. After taking the offering, my husband stood up and said, "I don't think we're through. I think the Lord wants us to also give a monthly pledge." So, the people started pledging.

Soon after the missionary evangelist returned to Russia, we got a phone call from him – and he was practically yelling over the phone! He kept shouting, "Dick, you just won't believe it!" He said, (and these were his exact words) "The love and hospitality your church showed us broke everything loose over here. We no sooner got back to Russia and the most perfect office space opened up, and guess what it cost -- the exact amount of your monthly pledge!!!" He went on to say that everything else started falling in place, as well -- the right staff, computers, office supplies, and everything they needed!

God was showing us how the Gift of Hospitality can even be used as a mighty weapon to tear down strongholds in the perilous end times that are upon us! The ways of God are marvelous, but we must follow his instructions, and then stand back and watch him fulfill his Word!

PRAYER – Lord, open doors for us to use the powerful Gift of Hospitality in these perilous end times to tear down strongholds, break through walls, and overcome the power of Satan operating in people's lives. Thank you for providing powerful weapons for God's people to use. AMEN~

She Ran The Marathon!

By Jeri Ingram

I can do all things through Christ which
strengthens me. Philippians 4:13 (KJV)

I once read a true story in Guideposts Magazine about a
25-year-old girl named Linda who was born with cerebral
palsy of the legs. She had to walk with canes strapped to both
her arms. She was very smart and held a Masters degree, but
she couldn't find a job. One day in 1982, as she was praying
about a job, the Lord spoke to her and said, "Run the New
York City marathon".

Naturally, she was shocked and had great reservations.
She felt it was an impossible goal. It was something only a
miracle could accomplish. But she decided that since God
had spoken to her, and scripture says that through Christ
we can do anything God has called us to do, that she would
attempt the run.

She faced incredible difficulties during the run, and she
shared in her story the ways in which God helped her. She
was so slow on her crutches that she was far behind all the
other runners, and by the time she reached the official water
stations, they had already been dismantled. But she just kept

saying over and over, "I can do all things through Christ who strengthens me."

As she reached the more dangerous neighborhoods in New York, people offered to walk with her as she ran, and others refilled her small water canteen so she could drink.

Late in the day as it began growing dark, she found herself totally alone, and she worried that she would no longer be able to see the blue line on the street showing the direction to go. She kept saying over and over, "I can do all things through Christ who strengthens me."

Just as the blue line was disappearing in the dark, an ABC camera crew showed up and asked to accompany her so she wouldn't get lost!

She did complete the marathon and later was invited to the White House! Named Athlete of the Year by the Cerebral Palsy Foundation, she appeared on many TV shows. She was also offered a job with the United Way of Tri-State in New York!

By making the decision to follow God's leading, she accomplished an impossible feat. The power of God was released in her life – and she got a job! That same power is available to anyone who will dare to believe!

PRAYER – Lord, as I face the challenges of the day, help me to remember that I do not have to rely on my own strength. The strength of God is always available to me. I just have to call on you, and you will give me your strength to do impossible things! AMEN

Why Pray?

By Jeri Ingram

My sheep listen to my voice; I know them,
and they follow me. John 10:27 (NIV)

We were born again less than a year before the Lord called us into the ministry. We decided to take a trip to Waxahachie, Texas, to see about attending the Christian university there. It was about a five-hour drive from where we lived.

It was a beautiful, sunshiny day when we left one morning with some friends. We were approximately halfway there, driving through the countryside with no other cars in sight, when I suddenly felt a strong prompting of the Lord to pray for safety. I couldn't see any imminent danger anywhere, but nevertheless, I began to quietly pray without saying a word to anyone in the car.

Suddenly, my husband pulled our car completely off the road and stopped. We were all surprised and asked him what he was doing. He said, "I don't know why, but I felt like the Lord was telling me to get off the road."

We sat there puzzled, when suddenly a large, 18-wheel truck came over the hill, driving *ON THE WRONG SIDE OF THE ROAD!*

As he whizzed by, we didn't know if the driver had fallen asleep or possibly was drinking, but if we had not heard and obeyed the still, small voice of the Lord, we would most certainly have had a head-on collision! I learned that day not to ignore those inner promptings. They can save your life!

PRAYER – Lord, help me today to listen and obey those still, small promptings that arise deep in my spirit. You are a loving God who takes care of His children and I thank you for it. AMEN

God Will Provide Your Seed

By Jeri Ingram

Now He who supplies seed to the Sower
and bread for food will also supply and
increase your store of seed and will
enlarge the harvest of your righteousness.
2 Corinthians 9:10 (NIV)

I remember the first time I ever felt led by the Lord to give a $1,000 offering. It was for a special need in Israel, and my heart soared with excitement to give to our beloved spiritual homeland. I had never given that much money in a single offering before, and the thought of sowing that amount into the land of our faith was glorious! There was just one problem -- I didn't have $1,000.

So, I went to the Lord in prayer. I told the Lord that it was my heart's desire to give, and it was my heart's desire to bless Israel, but I didn't have that amount of money. Then I reminded him of his promise to supply seed to the sower and asked if he would provide the $1,000 for me to give.

A few days went by, and nothing happened. Then Sunday came and we went to church. Before church began we were in my husband's office preparing for service when someone knocked on the door. When I opened the door, there was an usher with an envelope in his hands. He handed the envelope directly to me and said, "This is for you."

The envelope had my name written on the front, but nothing else. There was no note on the inside to indicate who it was from. The only thing I found in the envelope was $1,200 in cash. It took my breath away! I knew it was God's provision for my offering to Israel.

Thanking God for supernaturally supplying seed, I immediately put $1,000 in an offering envelope for Israel. I took the remaining $200 and put it in my husband's hand saying, "Here, honey! It's a little gift from God & me to you!" We both laughed & thanked God for His amazing faithfulness.

That was my first time to ever give an offering of that amount. Since that time God has asked me to give an offering like that many times. I always get excited to watch how God will provide what I need in order to obey his instructions. He has never, ever failed!

PRAYER – Lord, I thank you for the privilege of giving. It's an honor to sow into your Kingdom, and a great thrill to see how you provide the seed for me to sow. I thank you for your faithfulness! AMEN

The Power Of The Blood

By Jeri Ingram

When I see the blood, I will pass over you,
and the plagues shall not be upon you to
destroy you when I smite the land of Egypt.
Exodus 12:13 (KJV)

It was a Wednesday night church service, and I was leading the congregation in a time of corporate prayer. Normally I would do something like have the people stand together and pray, or possibly even hold hands together and pray. But that night I felt led to have them do something that I had never done before. I asked them to form a circle all around the sanctuary, hold hands, and simultaneously begin to plead the blood of Jesus over the whole building. I had no idea why we needed to do that, but I knew to obey that inner prompting.

The next morning one of our pastors was the first to arrive at the church. When he opened the front door and walked in, he was greeted by an overwhelming smell of natural gas. Someone had accidentally left the stove on in the kitchen in the Fellowship Hall, and gas had permeated the whole building, even filling the adjoining sanctuary. He got the gas turned off and opened all the windows and doors to air it out.

I believe if we had not invited the blood of Jesus to cover the building, there could have been an explosion destroying property, and possibly even lives. There is incredible power in the blood of Jesus, and that power is available to us as believers. We just have to ask for it.

PRAYER – Lord, I ask you to cover my family today with the blood of Jesus. Cover us and protect us at home, at school, at work, in our cars, wherever we are. I thank you that the blood of your Son is as powerful today as it was when he was hanging on the Cross for our sakes. AMEN

Follow The Leading Of The Holy Spirit

By Jeri Ingram

For those who are led by the Spirit of God are
the children of God. Romans 8:14 (NIV)

We lived in a small mobile home on the campus of the Christian University my husband was attending. One warm summer day I was sitting on the couch folding laundry in the living room. The couch where I was sitting was right next to the front door, and on the other side was the front porch where Kimberly, our three-year-old daughter, was playing. She loved to sit and play on that porch with her dolls. She was no more than three feet away from me and I could easily reach her if she needed me, so she seemed perfectly safe, but I began to feel an urgency to pray for her safety.

I looked out the door to check on her, and she was fine, but about five minutes later, I heard her give a blood-curdling scream. I flew to the door and to my horror I saw that she had fallen down the steps to the rock sidewalk below and was lying on the ground, face down. I scooped her up and held her close. After her sobbing subsided, I began to check her out for injuries. To my amazement there were no injuries at all – not even any scratches. The fall had merely scared her, and as soon as she was through crying, she wanted to go right back to playing.

I am convinced if the Lord hadn't given me that nudge to pray for her safety, that she would have been hurt – perhaps seriously. How crucially important it is to follow the leading of the Holy Spirit in every situation. It can mean life or death!

PRAYER – Lord, I pray that you will help me be sensitive to your leading today. Please speak to me clearly and unmistakably so I can understand, and I pray that I will always hear your voice and obey whatever you ask. I ask this in the lovely name of Jesus. AMEN

If It Matters To You, It Matters To God

By Jeri Ingram

Through knowledge its rooms are
filled with rare and beautiful treasures.
Proverbs 24:4 (NIV)

When we moved from Texas to Rhode Island to pioneer a church, we brought only clothes, linens and dishes with us. Everything else we sold or gave away before we left our lifelong home of Texas. Slowly, we gathered some furniture and practical items to make our new home functional, but we had absolutely nothing to make it warm and inviting – not even one single picture to hang on the wall.

As a wife and mother, I felt it was my responsibility to make our home warm, comfortable and inviting – a haven for our family. So, I went to prayer and asked the Lord to help me fulfill that responsibility.

A short time later I received a catalogue in the mail filled with beautiful home decorations. I loved everything in the book, however, it was Christmas time and, as new pioneer pastors, we didn't have extra money.)

One day as I sat looking through the catalogue, the scripture began going through my mind over and over, "Give and it shall be given unto you." Luke 6:38 (KJV) I knew the Lord was showing me what to do. I quickly grabbed the catalogue and began choosing different items for each one of our relatives for Christmas. It was wonderful to choose items that would fit the individual taste and décor of each of their homes. It was also exciting to know that each gift was a seed I was planting toward eventually decorating our own home. I couldn't stop thanking God, and I decided not to share my act of faith with anyone.

Within a few short months, out of the blue we began receiving gifts from various people. We were given beautiful pictures, curtains, knickknacks, and decorations that filled our home and made it more beautiful than I could ever have done on my own. It was the goodness and generosity of God!

Several years later, we moved into a new home and some of our church members were there helping us pack. The dining table was covered with knickknacks and beautiful things ready to be packed. One of the men looked at the table and jokingly said, "You could open a gift store with all these things." I replied, "Those were gifts! They were gifts the Lord gave us because we obeyed his Word about giving."

God desires to take care of his children, and he left us instructions. All we have to do is love him with all our hearts and follow his instructions. It's that simple!

PRAYER – Lord, I thank you for caring about every single area of our lives. You said, "'The just shall live by faith,'"

Romans 1:17 (KJV) and that includes everything -- food, clothing, health, relationships, our homes -- everything! I thank you that nothing is too small or too great for our faith to move the hand of God! AMEN

Happy Anniversary!

By Jeri Ingram

Seek ye first the Kingdom of God and his
righteousness; and all these things shall be
added unto you. Matthew 6:33 (KJV)

It was our wedding anniversary and we wanted to celebrate, but we had no money. We were poor college students, and we had only one pack of American cheese in the refrigerator and one can of peas in the cupboard. That was it!

All we knew was we loved God with all our hearts and we trusted him to take care of us. Our girls were both little and loved to play at the park, so we decided that would be a fun place to take them for the day. We would celebrate our anniversary by being together and enjoying each other. We prayed together before we left, and told God we trusted him to provide for us. Then we went to the park and had a wonderful day!

Later that afternoon, as we returned and pulled up to our little mobile home on campus, our eyes popped! There on the front porch were bags and bags of groceries. They were literally wall to wall! We had not told anyone but the Lord of our financial situation, so we were shocked. We brought the bags in the house and went through them. There were groceries there to meet every need – even baby food. We were so overjoyed we couldn't stop thanking God over and over!!!

As we were standing there thanking God for his blessings, two of our neighbors knocked on our door. They both knew that it was our anniversary and had decided to go together and bless us on our special day. They had started by filling our porch with the bags of groceries, and then they told us that they had cooked us dinner for our anniversary and wanted to bring it over. We were speechless!

So, they left and then came back with a fabulous dinner. They insisted that our family sit down at the table and let them serve us. We felt as though angels were serving us and we could hardly hold back the tears. After we had finished the wonderful meal, they brought out the grand finale -- a Baked Alaska! Wow! With flames leaping up off the tall meringue, it was much more than a dessert - it was an experience!!!!

After dinner was over, our sweet neighbors insisted that they wash the dishes and clean up the kitchen while we put our two little girls to bed. Talk about going the *EXTRA MILE*!

The whole experience was so special and heartwarming, but even more significantly, it was a clear demonstration and reminder to us of the love and care God shows to his beloved children when they put him first in their lives!!

PRAYER – Lord, I thank you today for your great love for us, and I commit myself afresh and anew to love and serve you with all my heart. AMEN

God Can Take Care
Of His Children

By Jeri Ingram

You will drink from the brook,
and I have directed the ravens to
supply you with food there. I Kings 17:4 (NIV)

While attending Southwestern Assemblies of God University, my husband took an extra heavy course load. In fact, he completed four years of college in three year's time. During that time he also worked part-time in construction while I was at home with a toddler and a newborn. We were like most of the other couples on campus -- poor college students! Finances were sparse. Despite the lack of finances, though, it was amazing how God took care of us!

One morning my husband and I were praying together before he left for class. We were at a place where we needed some supernatural intervention from the Lord. We had bills that were due and we desperately needed to buy some groceries. We told the Lord what we needed and thanked him for his loving care and provision.

As my husband was leaving for class, he noticed an envelope stuck under the windshield wipers. He opened it, and inside were several one-hundred-dollar bills! There was no name on the envelope, nor any note inside. We had not told our need to anyone but the Lord, and we never did find out who our benefactor was, but we knew it was clearly an answer to the prayer we had just prayed earlier that morning.

Over and over during those three years of college, the Lord provided for us in supernatural ways, showing his love and care for us. His promise to care for his children is true! Don't be afraid to step out into the unknown. You can TRUST him!!!!!!

PRAYER – Lord, what a joy and a privilege to serve a God like you, who truly cares for his children! I ask you today to provide our needs according to all your riches in glory, and I thank you in advance in the lovely name of our Savior, Jesus Christ! AMEN

Riots On Dowling Street!!

By Jeri Ingram

A thousand may fall at your side, ten thousand
at your right hand, but it will not come near
you. Psalm 91:7 (NIV)

It was 1970 and my husband was working as a Houston
police officer. We had been born-again Christians for
almost a year and were preparing to move to Waxahachie,
Texas, to attend a Christian university there in preparation
for entering the ministry.

One Sunday night we attended church and arrived home
unusually late. It was around 11:00 pm as we walked in
the door and the phone was ringing. It was the police
department calling to tell Dick that riots had broken out
on Dowling Street in the center of Houston. The Black
Panther gang members had literally taken control of several
streets in the downtown area, and police were trying to
regain control. They were calling all off-duty policemen
to gather all the arms they could find and get down to the
department ASAP!

It was chilling news!

As Dick quickly changed into his uniform, I sat on the side of the bed reading Psalm 91:7 (KJV), *out loud*, over and over, "A thousand may fall at your side, and 10,000 may fall at your right hand, but it shall not come near you". We prayed a quick prayer together for his safety, and *all* the police officers' safety, then he was out the door.

As soon as he left, I called his mom, my mom, and a few friends I knew who knew how to really pray. Then I went into the living room and began praying, also.

As I prayed, the Lord gave me instructions. I clearly heard his still, small voice in my spirit saying something that shocked me. He impressed me to pray that the leader of the gang would be *killed!* It took my breath away, and I felt a little lightheaded. I had *never* prayed that someone would be killed! But God said, "Do it" -- so I did!

At 5:00 am the next morning Dick called me and said, "It's over!" What a relief! He said it was the most unbelievable thing he had ever seen. The streets of Houston, a huge, cosmopolitan city, were lit up with sporadic gunfire flashes, looking like a war zone. He said during the firefight one of the police sharpshooters was able to get an aim on the leader of the gang and shot and wounded him. He died shortly thereafter at Ben Taub Hospital. Within minutes, the word spread that their leader was dead, and the gang members began to retreat. Their organized riot fell apart. The Lord, in his sovereign wisdom, understood exactly what was needed to resolve that desperate situation.

Dick said even in the midst of all the gunfire, not one policeman was hurt, not even a scratch! We could not stop thanking and praising God!!!

The Lord proved once again we can trust him to fulfill his promises, even in the direst of circumstances!

PRAYER – Lord, I thank you for your promise of protection for those who trust in you. I ask you today to watch over every member of my family as they go their separate ways and bring us all back safely together at the end of the day. Thank you for your divine protection. AMEN

Let God Direct You

By Jeri Ingram

Whether you turn to the right or to the
left, your ears will hear a voice behind
you saying, This is the way; walk in it.
Isaiah 30: 21-23 (NIV)

Through the years we have done a lot of traveling and have stayed at many hotels & motels – some good, some not so good. Only once, though, did we ever have an unusual experience like the following story ...

We had been traveling for days. Our girls were young and *so* ready to be out of the car! It was hot and they especially wanted a swim, so we stopped at a nice hotel with a large swimming pool in the middle of the complex. The girls were excited and we were all looking forward to a refreshing and relaxing time. We checked into the hotel and carried our bags to the hotel room, laughing and talking and ready to get into our swimsuits.

As we walked into the room, however, I instantly felt a dramatic change in the atmosphere. One minute I had felt happy and jovial, and in a flash as I entered the room, I felt enveloped by a strange, heavy, oppressive, and dark feeling. I instinctively felt certain that some kind of terrible death had taken place in the room. The feeling was stifling. I didn't say anything because I didn't want to scare the girls, but I started praying under my breath for God's protection and guidance.

The next minute my husband said, "You know what, girls, I don't think I like this room. Let's go see if we can get something better." We went to the desk and asked for something else and they changed us to a room on the opposite side of the complex. The room was perfect, with a light and peaceful atmosphere.

We stayed at the hotel for two days and had a wonderful time. My husband (a former policeman) told me later that he didn't say anything at the time so he wouldn't scare us, but he felt certain that a murder had taken place in that first room.

I don't know if anything bad would have happened if we had stayed in the first room, but I do know that God loves us enough to watch over us and protect us from demonic encounters by leading us by his Spirit out of harm's way! All we must do is '*listen and obey*'.

PRAYER – Lord, I pray that you will help me be sensitive to your still, small voice all day today. Give me the grace to listen and then obey, for I know that is the only true protection we have in these troubled times. Thank you for your love and your care. AMEN

Teach Your Children To Pray

By Jeri Ingram

Let us, your servants, see you work
again; let our children see your glory.
Psalm 90:16 (NLT)

While my husband was attending Southwestern Assemblies of God University, we lived on campus in the trailer park designated for married couples. Our oldest daughter, Kimberly, was three years old, and our youngest, Kristina, was a newborn infant. All the children living around us were school age, so there were no playmates for our very active and social three-year-old.

My husband and I were always looking for ways to show our children how good God is and how much he loves them, so I decided to turn the situation into a prayer challenge for our little daughter. I immediately went to her and began to explain my exciting new plan to pray that God would send her a friend who would live right next door to us so they could go to each other's homes to play together, even in bad weather.

She excitedly began to jump up and down and clap her hands, and we began our prayer challenge with a high sense of expectation. Every morning we would kneel together in front of the living room couch and pray that God would send a friend for Kimberly – right next door!!

One fall day, a couple of weeks before school started, we looked out the window and saw the trailer next door to ours pulling out. We ran out to speak to the owners of the trailer to see where they were going. They were older than most of the couples in the trailer park and had decided to leave and go a different direction in their lives.

That left an empty trailer space right next door to us, so we began to watch expectantly for a new trailer to pull in. Every day we thanked God for answering our prayer, even though it hadn't happened yet. Day after day we prayed and thanked God, believing the answer was on the way.

Fall arrived, classes began, and the space next to our trailer remained empty. We kept praying and thanking God, but nothing happened. When college classes had been in session around a month and the space was still empty, I went to the Lord in prayer. I poured my heart out and told the Lord how I was using this prayer challenge to increase my daughter's faith. I wanted her to see that prayer works, and that God cares about us. I asked him what was causing the delay?

I remember the exact words he spoke to my heart. With great tenderness and love he said, "It is not expedient for me to send them right now, but at the appointed time they will arrive."

Expedient -- that word stood out to me, and my heart exploded with excitement!! I ran to tell Kimberly the good news. I told her we would no longer be praying for an answer; we would only be thanking God because God had promised the answer was already on the way! So, for the next couple of weeks we thanked God every morning that the answer was on the way.

And then it happened. One morning as Kimberly and I were in the living room praying together, we heard the loud noise of a truck. We both jumped up and ran to look out the window. There was a truck pulling a trailer into the empty space right next door. We stood watching, barely breathing, waiting to see who was moving in.

As the truck doors opened, a family of four began to pile out -- first the mother, then the father holding a little boy, and then last, a little girl climbed out! She was exactly Kim's height, had blond hair with a ponytail and bangs, just like Kim's. They looked like sisters!

I looked at Kim with a big smile on my face. With wide eyes, she turned without a word and walked out the front door. She went down the stairs and strode purposefully toward the little girl. Without a word, she took her hand and they walked off to go play, as if they had always known each other. I couldn't wipe the smile off my face!

Later, we found out her name was Julie, and they were only three weeks apart in age. We also learned they were from Chicago and had to sell their home and business before they could leave town, which explained the delay. Sometimes, when we are asking God for something, we forget that he must arrange things on the other end, so that all things are 'expedient'.

We lived in that trailer park for three more years, and Kim and Julie were inseparable. They played together almost every day, even in bad weather. Over time, occasionally Kimberly would say to me, "Remember when we prayed for a friend, and God sent Julie?" It was a clear visual for our three-year-old to see God's glory at work. It has remained one of our special memories.

If you are a parent, I would encourage you – don't wait to begin teaching your children how wonderful God is. In fact, I would say – the younger, the better. The younger they are, the easier they learn. Ask God to show you how to teach them and he will open doors for you. Don't miss your opportunity!

PRAYER – Lord, I pray that you will open my eyes to opportunities to help my children learn about you. Your Word declares that if we train up our children correctly, they won't depart from those ways. Help me to find real and tangible ways to show them how wonderful you are and how much you love them. Thank you for your help. AMEN

There Is Power In The
Name Of Jesus

By Jeri Ingram

Submit yourselves therefore to God. Resist
the devil, and he will flee from you.
James 4:7 (KJV)

While pastoring a church in the state of Rhode Island,
the Women's Ministries of our church decided to publish
a church cookbook as a fund raiser. I searched and found a
publishing company that could help us. I called and made
an appointment for a representative to come and give a
presentation to our ladies, so she came one night and spoke
at our church.

She lived in Connecticut and was going to drive back that
night after the meeting, but weather reports said a bad
snowstorm was approaching. My husband was out of town
and I was concerned for her to drive back to Connecticut
late at night in such bad weather, so I invited her to stay at
our home for the night. We all went home after the meeting,
went to bed and promptly fell asleep.

I had been sleeping soundly for a few hours when suddenly
I awoke with a start. I woke up to a stifling feeling of fear
in my room. The atmosphere was so heavy and oppressive I

felt paralyzed. I couldn't seem to move no matter how hard I tried. I couldn't speak -- my mouth just wouldn't open. I couldn't understand what was happening, and the only thing I could think to do was to try and say … *Jesus!*

At first, I had to just say his name in my mind because my mouth wouldn't open to speak. So, silently I kept saying his name to myself, over and over, until eventually, I could open my mouth just a little and whisper his name softly. Finally, my voice became stronger, and I began loudly saying … *JESUS,* over and over. The more I spoke his name, the oppressive feeling of fear in my room began to dissipate. Finally, everything returned to normal, and I knew Jesus had cleared my room of that evil presence, so I rolled over and went back to sleep peacefully for the rest of the night.

The next morning, I went downstairs to make breakfast for our guest, and I was surprised to see her already up and dressed, sitting in the living room waiting for me. It was obvious she was very excited about something. She breathlessly began saying, "You won't believe what happened to me last night! In the middle of the night my mother, who has been dead for ten years, appeared to me. She sat in the rocking chair at the foot of my bed and talked to me for over an hour."

I was stunned! No wonder I had felt the presence of evil in our house that night. Our guest had been talking to the dead! Before she left, I spent a long time talking to her about salvation and the love of God, then we never saw her again.

After she was gone, I couldn't stop thinking about what had happened. There were many thoughts flying around in my mind, but the foremost thought, and the one that has stayed with me all these years, is the power that was released simply by using *THE NAME OF JESUS.*

The spirit of fear in my room that night was real and strong, stronger than I was! But when I began to say his name over and over and over, power was released. God's power is stronger than any force, and the demonic force that wanted to overcome me had to flee. It couldn't stay in the presence of *HIS NAME!*

I want to encourage you, even in these *perilous end times* with bizarre things happening almost every day, that you do NOT need to be afraid. *THE NAME OF JESUS* is above every name, and his power and strength are greater than any force in the entire universe. You can trust him! Just say his name, and demons will flee before you!!!!

PRAYER – Lord, the power in your name is so amazing. And even more amazing is the fact that you allow us, your children, to use your name in our ordinary, earthly situations. Help us to never forget that you have been given all authority in Heaven and on earth, and you have given those who call you their Savior the right to use that name to conquer the power of darkness. AMEN

The Merriest Christmas!

By Jeri Ingram

If anyone has material possessions and sees
a brother or sister in need but has no pity
on them, how can the love of God be in
that person? I John 3:17 (NIV)

There was a dry cleaners close to our house where I took
our clothes for cleaning. Several of the clerks working
there were from Brazil. They were all lovely girls with cute
personalities, and I enjoyed talking with them whenever I
went into the store.

Over time I got to know them and some of their personal
stories. In talking with one of the girls, I learned she was
married with children, even a baby. She had left her children
and baby with her mother and husband, who was a security
guard, while she came to America alone to make money to
send back to her family in Brazil. Her story broke my heart.
I couldn't imagine being separated from my family and my
baby, and I found myself praying for them and asking God
how I could help them.

It was the Christmas season and one day she was talking
about how hard it was to not see her children during the
holiday season. Immediately I felt the Lord place it in my

heart to buy Christmas presents for her to send to her children, so I asked her the age and gender of each child.

That weekend I took my ten-year-old granddaughter, Kaylee, along with me as my expert gift advisor. We got a huge basket and went down the aisle choosing age-appropriate gifts. My granddaughter had as much fun as I did and was an invaluable help as we carefully picked toys and games for each child. The next day my heart filled with joy as I presented the gifts, along with some money for shipping, to the lovely Brazilian girl at the cleaners. The look of gratitude on her face was priceless!

The Bible says "It is more blessed to give than to receive" *Acts. 20:35 (NIV)*, and I certainly experienced it that day. The joy of giving to children and their mother who would not see each other on Christmas Day was indescribable!

We should ask the Lord to always help us stay alert to people in need, and for ways to give and help make their burdens lighter. There is no greater peace, joy or satisfaction, and it truly shows the *HEART OF GOD* to a hurting world!

PRAYER – Lord, in all the business of life today, please help me to remember to watch for people who need something to remind them how much God loves them. Bring people across my pathway that I can share the love of God and heal their hurting hearts. AMEN

Called Together

By Jeri Ingram

And he said unto them, go ye into all the
world and preach the gospel to every creature.
Mark 16:15 (KJV)

My husband and I were both twenty-six years old and
had been born-again less than a year. We were excited,
turned-on Christians! In fact, we often commented to each
other how we literally felt *'on fire'* with the love and power
of God! All we wanted to do was share with others the
wonderful, marvelous, amazing thing God had done in our
lives. Even so, we were still totally surprised by what God
did in our lives one Sunday night at church.

The service was wonderful, as always. We worshipped, we
praised, we rejoiced, and we enjoyed the anointed preaching
of the Word. At the end of the service, we went to the altar,
got on our knees, and prayed together. It was glorious! The
longer we prayed, the more intense and real the presence of
God became.

Suddenly the atmosphere became charged with the Holy
Spirit, like a glory spout was poured out over us. I have never
experienced anything so intense in my life. The force of it
was so strong I felt my head pushed down till my forehead

was touching the altar. I was weeping so hard under the weight of God's love I could scarcely get my breath.

I began to see a vision. I saw myself surrounded by children and I was handing out pieces of bread to each one of them. I instinctively knew the bread represented the Word of God and the children represented people who were hungry for knowledge of their Heavenly Father!

I became aware of my husband kneeling beside me, weeping as hard as I was. He turned and looked at me, and through tears said, "God has just called me into the ministry!" Through my own tears I replied, "God just called me into the ministry, also!" At that, we fell into each other's arms and continued weeping on each other's shoulder.

After leaving church that night, we knew we were different. We had accepted the 'Call of God' to preach the gospel. We were excited and humbled, and we knew our lives would never be the same!

From there, we set out to follow the God of the universe, allowing Him to direct our lives and our ministry, and we have never regretted that decision!

PRAYER – Lord, I believe every person has a destiny that you prepared for their lives. Help me to be sensitive and obedient to fulfill your plan and purpose for my life. AMEN

Big Or Small -- God Meets Every Need!

By Jeri Ingram

My God will meet all your needs according
to the riches of his glory in Christ Jesus.
Philippians 4 :19 (NIV)

It was fall and the weather was just beginning to turn
cool. I looked outside and saw our three year old daughter,
Kimberly, running through the grass barefooted. I was
concerned because she had outgrown her old tennis shoes
and would need a new pair quickly as the weather was
already changing from summer to fall; but being college
students with two children and only a part-time job, we just
didn't have the money to buy any.

So, I went to prayer and reminded God of his promise to
meet all our needs according to his riches in glory; I told
him we had a real need for shoes for our toddler and asked
him to provide that need. I thanked him for hearing and
answering my prayer.

That afternoon I was in town and I stopped in front of
the department store on Main Street. There was a pair of
tiny red tennis shoes in the window marked $4 plus some

change. I asked the Lord to provide a way for us to buy them and then went home.

The next day when I brought in the mail there was a letter from a lady in our home town whom we had not seen since we left for college. I opened the letter and there it was, a check for $5.00! She apologized for sending such a small amount but said the Lord had clearly spoken to her to send us a check for that amount.

I immediately got in the car and went to the store and bought the shoes. As I placed the shoes on Kimberly later that day, I told her they were a gift from Jesus, and we thanked God together. She was so excited!

Sometimes I think people hesitate to ask God for things that seem too small, but God truly cares about ALL our needs -- big or small!!!

PRAYER – Lord, how can we ever thank you enough for your great love for us. Thank you for always meeting our needs, no matter how big or how small they may be. We are so grateful for your loving care. AMEN

A Special Assignment

By Jeri Ingram

I will bless those who bless Israel.
Genesis 12:3 (NIV)

Sharon, Massachusetts is the town in which we served as pastors for twenty-six years before retiring. It had at least seven Jewish synagogues, with a population of only 17,000 people, and it was referred to by some as *'America's Little Jerusalem.'*

In the beginning of our ministry there, we rented a van and took our intercessors with us to drive through Sharon each week, praying over every home, every school, every business, every church, and especially every Jewish temple. We did this for an entire year!

As a church, we felt our primary vision was to take the message of Christ's love to every person possible in Sharon, to every surrounding town, and to all the world. We also, however, felt God placed us in this strategic location with a 'special assignment' to show God's love to our Jewish friends.

Over the years, we were able to develop friendships with several of the Jewish rabbis in Sharon. We often visited their synagogues for special events, and we invited them to our church in return. Some did visit our church from time to time, and our congregation was always blessed by the opportunity to show them hospitality and honor as God's chosen people!

One young Jewish man, surprised by the love and respect we demonstrated, said with feeling, "I didn't think people like you liked people like us." He seemed moved and touched by the genuine care we showed them.

Once, we hosted a community event called *'A Winter Concert'* where we asked local protestant churches and Jewish temples to bring their choirs to our church for the special event. We asked each choir to sing individually, and then come together as a community choir for the final song. It was beautiful!

Afterwards, we offered refreshments in the Fellowship Hall. It was beautifully decorated with the Jewish colors of blue and white, and there were sparkly icicles hanging from the ceiling. We even had one table filled with kosher foods to make our Jewish friends feel welcome!

There was a wonderful feeling of warmth and fellowship all evening. As our Jewish friends were leaving, many stopped to tell us this was their first time in a protestant church and, with faces glowing, they told us how they felt such love and warmth the whole evening. We felt the pleasure of God on the whole event, and made many friends in the Jewish community.

One year our church celebrated *JERUSALEM DAY* and placed a banner on the front grounds of the church announcing the event. Early the next morning we received a call from the police!

Vandals had painted swastikas on the doors of the church, and they threw a very large rock through the window of the church office, shattering the windowpane and the glass top of my husband's desk.

News quickly spread through the Jewish community and one of the rabbis came immediately to help our church members with cleanup and repair. We were amazed and blessed to receive letters of support and encouragement from Jews everywhere – even letters from rabbis and Jews in Israel!

A faithful member of our church cleaned up the offending rock and painted a scripture onto it that said, "No weapon that is formed against you will succeed!" Isaiah 54:17 (AMP). That was our declaration, so we placed the rock prominently on the Communion table at the front of the sanctuary! It served to remind people of the greatness and the goodness of our God!

One Sunday, a rabbi dropped by our church in the middle of a church service. The rabbi stopped an usher in the lobby to tell him that it was widely known among the Jewish people in Boston that our church was supportive of them, and they wanted to say thank you!

Yes, there have been a few negative responses to our support of the Jews, but the blessings and joy we received for supporting Israel have been far greater!

PRAYER – Lord, as believers we consider it an honor to pray for your chosen people, the Jews, and we earnestly pray for the peace of Jerusalem as you have commanded. You promised to bless those who bless Israel and it is our privilege to do so. AMEN

I Love Bling!

By Jeri Ingram

> The wall was made of jasper, and the city of
> pure gold, as pure as glass. The foundations
> of the city walls were decorated with every
> kind of precious stone. The first foundation
> was jasper, the second sapphire, the third
> agate, the fourth emerald, the fifth onyx, the
> sixth ruby, the seventh chrysolite, the eighth
> beryl, the ninth topaz, the tenth turquoise,
> the eleventh jacinth, and the twelfth amethyst.
> The twelve gates were twelve pearls, each gate
> made of a single pearl. The great street of the
> city was of gold, as pure as transparent glass.
> Revelation 21: 18-21 (NIV)

I have always loved sparkly, shiny things. I guess you could
say I come by it naturally. My 5' 2" mother, the cutest,
funniest person you would ever want to meet, loved sparkly,
shiny things. Her favorite pair of shoes were gold metallic
tennis shoes. She wore them proudly despite all the joking
and teasing we gave her about them.

But aside from my natural affinity for sparkle, I believe
there is also a deeper reason. I am a believer! Heaven is my
home, and when I read the Bible about the heavenly city, it
knocks my socks off. Heaven is decorated with every kind

181

of beautiful jewel and stone there is. Each gate is one single huge pearl. And the light of God's Son, Jesus Christ, shines so brilliantly that it is never night. It makes me tingly with reverent wonder just thinking about it all. I used to playfully tell our congregation that I love bling because it reminds me of the glorious sparkle and glow of heaven!

When my girls were little, I used to let my imagination run wild when talking to them about heaven. I would tell them that since the Bible says the streets are beautiful with pure, shiny gold, I was pretty sure there was probably enough extra gold to build beautiful, shiny, gold swing sets for little boys and girls to swing on. I would talk about how everything there sparkles with all the different jewels.

Heaven is a real place. We must choose Christ while we're still here on earth if we want to go there, so I wanted them to have a picture in their minds of heaven that was so glorious and magnificent they would not fear it, but instead look forward with great anticipation to that day when they get to move into their fabulous mansion in that glorious city!

To me, that is the sacred responsibility of a parent, to find appropriate ways to move, prompt, stimulate, induce, activate, propel, arouse, inspire and motivate our children to make the greatest decision of their lives – to love God and make heaven their eternal home!!!

PRAYER – Lord, please give me creative ideas today of ways I can help my children to understand and believe how glorious heaven is! By your grace, please help me find ways to help them to have no fear, but only excitement and anticipation about their future heavenly home. AMEN

Guard Your Heart

By Jeri Ingram

Guard your heart above all else, for
it determines the course of your life.
Proverbs 4:23 (NLT)

One Sunday we were having a powerful worship service.
The presence of the Lord was very real. I was standing on
the platform beside my husband, worshipping God, when
my eyes fell upon a man who had been attending our church
with his wife for many years. It was like the Lord suddenly
gave me x-ray vision to see inside his body. I could clearly
see his heart, and I was startled to see that his heart looked
unmistakably like a hard stone. I found myself weeping in
sorrow for him.

I felt impressed by the Lord to go out in the congregation
and speak to him. Everyone was still worshipping, standing
with eyes closed and hands raised in surrender to the Lord,
so I quietly slipped into the seat next to the man with no
one noticing.

I gently tapped his arm and asked to speak to him. I told him
the vision the Lord had shown me of his hard, stony heart,
and that the Lord loved him and wanted to soften his heart
so he could freely love again. He began sobbing violently!

He sobbed and sobbed, and I sat softly praying until he gained composure.

I asked if I could pray for God to heal him and set him free and soften his heart. He stared at me a long time, then muttered something under his breath, got up and stomped out. I knew he was refusing God's loving offer. It was heartbreaking!

Not too long after that his wife suddenly became ill and died, and he moved away. The last report I heard of him was that he had stopped attending church and was living with a woman out of wedlock. He totally turned his back on God!

It is a tragic story, but it is also a poignant reminder of the outstretched arms of love that God continually offers to us, while at the same time always allowing us the free will of making our own choices. He loves us all the time, but it is up to us to guard our hearts and keep them free of hatred, unforgiveness, bitterness, or anything else that would cause it to become hard and unfeeling toward the love of God. Above all else – guard your heart!

PRAYER – Lord, I pray today that you will reveal to me anything in my heart that would prevent your love from flowing freely to me and through me to others. AMEN

The Pure Joy Of Giving

By Jeri Ingram

It is more blessed to give than to receive.
Acts 20:35 (NIV)

My father-in-law was one of the sweetest, most generous Christians I have ever known. It was obvious that giving to others truly brought him more enjoyment than anything else he did in life.

One year he sold some property he had inherited from his father. Instead of hoarding the money to himself, he gladly shared portions of it with his sisters. Next, he called us in Waxahachie, where we were living while my husband attended Bible College. Knowing college students don't usually have extra money for entertainment, he decided he wanted to bless us and our friends who lived in the little trailer park designated for married students on campus. It was his way of showing his gratefulness to God for the financial blessing.

When he called, he told my husband to get all our friends together because he wanted to take us to a renowned steak house in Dallas, well-known for its delicious steaks. That night there were about thirty of us seated around a long table, and the excitement and sheer glee among the college students as they ate those fabulous steaks was undeniable.

There was a lot of laughter as some were trying to decide if they should save one last bite of the delectable meat so they could frame it and hang it on the wall. It was obviously a time of refreshing and encouragement to those hardworking students who had dedicated their lives to service for the Lord.

The whole time we were all savoring the rare treat, Dick's dad sat at the end of the table just watching. He never ate a bite. He just sat there with tears pouring down his cheeks the whole time. It was obvious that the joy he was experiencing from giving to others meant much more to him than eating a steak. I thought of Jesus' words when he said, "I have meat to eat that you know not of." John 4:32 (KJV).

My father-in-law was one of those silent heroes that never liked to draw attention to himself, but tirelessly helped others. He regularly drove cancer patients to the hospital for treatment, weekly mowed the yards of all the widows in our church, and so much more. He was an inspiration to everyone who knew him, and truly displayed the truth of Acts 20:35 (NIV), "It is more blessed to give than to receive". He set an example to follow that would make all of our lives more joyful and fulfilled.

PRAYER – Lord, I pray that today you will open doors for me to spread your love to people who need reminders of how much God loves them. Give me creative ideas of how to bless people in the most effective ways. Let me be the hands and feet of Jesus while I'm here on the earth. AMEN

God Translated Us

By Jeri Ingram

> "…when they came up out of the water, the
> Spirit of the Lord snatched Philip away. The
> eunuch never saw him again but went on his
> way rejoicing." Acts 8:39 (NLT)

I have long believed that in the End Times there will be
miracles, signs and wonders greater than they saw in the
Early Church. In fact, the Bible tells us, "Greater works than
these shall you do" in John 14:12 (ASV)

One of the most fascinating stories in the Bible to me is found
in the eighth chapter of Acts where God led Phillip to the
eunuch to explain things he was reading in the scriptures.
After Phillip had clarified the scriptures to the eunuch and
baptized him, God translated him. He just snatched him
away and set him down again in a totally different location.
Amazing!

One time, as we were living in Rhode Island, we visited
my sister, Sarah, and her family in Connecticut. When we
returned home a few days later, we left late in the day. It had
been a wonderful, but tiring visit and we were exhausted.
We couldn't wait to get home and fall into bed.

We drove along in the dark, trying to stay awake and alert for the two-hour drive ahead of us. Suddenly, after only fifteen to twenty minutes of being on the road, we looked up and we were at the exit by our house. (I promise, we were NOT speeding!)

We were both shocked at how quickly we arrived home! After discussing it, we decided the only conclusion was that God had accelerated our trip. We felt like it was a little foretaste of things to come in the End Times – being translated, miracles, signs and wonders!!

Knowing God is the most exciting life anyone could ever live!!!

PRAYER – Lord, it is so exciting to serve a supernatural God like you! I pray that you will help me be sensitive to whatever you want to do in my life. I know that the invisible, supernatural realm where you dwell is more real than the visible, natural world where we live, and I want to be a part of whatever you are doing. AMEN

God Will Protect You

By Jeri Ingram

Deliver me from my enemies, O God; be my
fortress against those who are attacking me.
Psalm 59:1 (NIV)

We had always heard that new churches were sometimes
targeted for unusual attacks; probably the devil's attempt to
stop it before it ever gets started.

We were pioneering a new church in Rhode Island that
had recently moved into the top floor of an office building
complex, and we affectionately called it 'the upper room'.
One weekday morning my husband was about to leave for
the church when a neighboring pastor called and asked if he
could borrow our copy machine and asked if he could ride
with my husband to the church.

When they arrived at the church, the neighboring pastor
remained in the car while my husband went to unlock the
door. As he was bending over to unlock the door, a young
man we had briefly met only once or twice quietly slipped
up behind him wielding a 2 x 4 board, obviously planning
to bash my husband's head in. He didn't know, however, that
the neighboring pastor was sitting in the car.

When the neighboring pastor saw what was happening, he immediately jumped out of the car and yelled at the young man. It surprised and scared the young man, and he dropped the board and took off running. We had been warned to be careful of this young man as he was considered dangerous.

I am convinced that it was the Lord who caused that neighboring pastor to ride in the car with my husband that day. That was the only time he ever asked to do that, and it probably saved my husband's life.

I would like to encourage you that, no matter where the Lord calls you, or how dangerous it might be, God will find a way to help you. God truly delivers us from our enemies and protects us against those who want to attack us! You can trust Him!

PRAYER – Lord, I ask you today to protect me and protect my family. We entrust our lives into your care, and we thank you for your protection. AMEN

To Retire Or Not To Retire
-- That Is The Question!

By Jeri Ingram

There is a time for everything, and a
season for every activity under the heavens.
Ecclesiastes 3:1 (NIV)

We were in the ministry almost a half century and had no
desire to retire; in fact, we would gladly have continued in
the ministry until our last breath. My husband used to say
he wanted to die doing what he loved most – preaching in
the pulpit - although, I assured him, I felt pretty sure that
our congregation might not appreciate that so much!

Then my husband began to have issues with his health, and
it caused me to wonder if we might need to retire sooner
than we had hoped. Things that had always been easy, and
even enjoyable for him, became difficult and challenging.

I remembered an expression I learned while growing up
in Texas, *'you can tell when God is bringing change into your
life because He puts a burr under your saddle'*. This meant God
sometimes allows circumstances to become uncomfortable
as a motivating force for you to make the changes God
desires you to make.

My husband was in and out of the hospital, and each time I found myself wondering if it was time to retire, but each time I seemed to hear the Lord whispering, *"I'll tell you when."* I felt the Lord was letting me know that 'timing' was important in this decision.

Two years later, it became clear that retirement was necessary, and we prayed for the Lord to bring the couple of His choice to replace us in the ministry. There was a young minister and his wife we had known and loved for many years, and we learned they had been praying for the past two years about stepping down from their current ministry. The timing was perfect, for we were praying to step down at the same time they were praying to step into a new direction.

Circumstances came together quickly, and our long-time friends were installed as the new pastors of our church. The transition was smooth as glass, and the timing could not have been more perfect!

We had full confidence that God was leading and orchestrating the change, and even though the new pastor's style of ministry was totally different than ours, we felt their youth and giftings were appropriate for the current times. While we were called and anointed for the past generation, they were called and anointed for the next generation.

So, we retired. We were overwhelmed with gratitude at God's provision. The church named us Pastors Emeritus, for which we were so blessed and grateful. This allowed us to still be involved in the church and the ministry on a level we were able to comfortably fulfill.

Today the church is doing great! We watch with joy and gratitude to see the new pastors leading the church with the energy and creativity needed. Truly, God's timing is perfect. All we must do is be sensitive to his leading and he will work things out in the best way for everyone involved.

PRAYER – Father, help me to be sensitive to your timing in every area of my life. Help me constantly be aware that it is not only myself you are watching out for. There are other people involved that you care for as well. Give me the grace to wait patiently on your timing. AMEN

Our Last Chapter Together

By Jeri Ingram

My grace is sufficient for thee: for my
strength is made perfect in weakness.
2 Corinthians 12:9 (KJV)

We had just completed this book and were preparing to
send it to the publisher when the COVID-19 virus hit! With
the world-wide spread of the virus, everything changed.
We were all locked in our homes under quarantine. People
who dared go out on the streets were protesting, fighting,
vandalizing, tearing down beloved historical monuments
and displaying a total lack of respect and common sense.

Then the unthinkable happened, my husband was rushed to
the hospital with COVID-pneumonia. As the illness turned
into complication after complication, his days in the hospital
turned into months, and due to all the COVID restrictions,
he was quarantined and I was not allowed to visit him for
over three months! Other than his time in the military, we
had never been apart more than a few days at a time, so this
separation was hard.

Every day we would talk through a face-time app on our
cell phones that allowed us to see one another. We were

grateful to have that opportunity, and it did help, but it was definitely not the same as being together.

One day, shortly after hanging up from our daily phone call, I heard the Lord speak to me, and as clearly as I have ever heard his still, small voice, he said, "Hold on to my promises." I felt his presence and it was glorious. I wept tears of joy as his indescribable love wrapped around me like a warm blanket, and he began to give me scripture after scripture, which I immediately wrote down.

This visitation continued for *three weeks*, and when I typed up all the scriptures, I had five typewritten pages! I read them continually and kept saying over and over, "I trust you, Lord – I trust you!" Every time I said those words, I felt a surge of his Presence strengthen me. By the end of that three weeks, I was so filled with his Word that I felt stronger and more peaceful than I could ever remember. I was steady! My situation had not changed, but *I* had! Only God can do that, as we allow the power of his Holy Word to completely renew and recharge our minds!

Soon after that, a doctor surprisingly offered to allow Dick to come home -- with one condition -- we would need a hospital bed and a caregiver to help with his care.

For years, a very special Brazilian couple with a thriving cleaning business, Leandro and Celia, had been cleaning our house, and we had become very fond of them. Leandro was an unusually kind, energetic and caring man and was very resourceful and competent in many areas. As my daughters and I prayed about the right caregiver for my husband, we felt the Lord was leading us to ask Leandro. When he enthusiastically agreed, we were so grateful and couldn't stop thanking God for graciously meeting our need as he promised he would always do!

With Leandro's skillful caregiving help, I had the supreme joy and privilege of having my sweet husband at home for the next four months. We cared for him, and during those months he had the joy of being continually surrounded by all his family, which he loved with all his heart. On April 16, 2021, he peacefully slipped into the presence of the Lord.

When the hospice nurses arrived later after his passing, they told me they had never felt such a beautiful, peaceful atmosphere in a home that had just lost a loved one. The presence of God filled our house!!!!!!

After 56 years of a wonderful, fulfilling, and happy marriage, this could have been a devastating time for me, but instead, I experienced a level of God's grace beyond anything I had ever known.

Luke 8:11 describes the Word of God as a seed, and during the previous three-week visitation where God shared the scriptures with me, his promises were planted in the soil of my heart, and they produced a harvest of faith that literally turned my sorrow into joy. I felt joy that went deeper than the sorrow I felt at losing my lifelong sweetheart.

Soon after my husband's passing, I was telling the Lord how I missed the sweet company of my husband – just being able to sit and chat with him. I immediately heard the incredibly tender voice of God gently whisper in my ear, "I will be your husband." I wept tears of joy at the indescribable *COMFORT* and *PEACE* that flooded my heart.

Through all this, God's grace has been sufficient on a level I had never before experienced. God prepared and strengthened me for what lay ahead of me! I did not want my sweet husband to go, and I miss him every day, but truly, as I Thess.4:13 (KJV) says, "We sorrow not, even as others which have no hope." My husband is not here now, but I know I will see him again, and that fills me with great joy!

This was indeed the hardest experience of my lifetime, but it was also a time of deeper joy and peace than I have ever known. Through this time, I learned *GOD IS ENOUGH!!!!!!* If you put your trust in him, he can bring you through anything victoriously! But trust doesn't just happen automatically, you must press in and go after God with all your heart. James 4:8 (KJV) says, "Draw nigh to God and he will draw nigh to you."

The scriptures given to me during that three-week visitation helped me get my thoughts, my eyes, my heart and mind so fastened on the goodness of God and the faithfulness of His promises, that when it was time for my sweetheart to go, I had the grace I needed! I knew, beyond any shadow of doubt, that God was with me and was helping me. For the first time in my life, I understood what it meant to have peace that passes all understanding.

I learned you don't have to fear the future. In fact, you don't have to fear anything, for you can trust and rest in the fact that in our times of greatest weakness or deepest heartache, God's grace is sufficient to carry you through!!!!

PRAYER – God, I thank you for the gift of your Holy Word that is a lamp unto my feet and a light unto my path. I ask you today to lead and guide my thoughts, my words and my actions. I ask you to strengthen me in my weak times, and give me your grace to be victorious in any situation that comes my way, that your name might be glorified! AMEN

A Note To Parents

By Jeri Ingram

> Teach them (My words) to your children,
> talking about them when you sit at home and
> when you walk along the road, when you lie
> down and when you get up ... so that your
> days and the days of your children may be
> many in the land the Lord swore to give you.
> Deuteronomy 11:19, 20 (NIV)

In 3 John 1:4 (KJV), John made a statement that has been one of the greatest truths of our lives. He said, "I have no greater joy than to hear that my children are walking in the truth." He was profoundly correct!

Both of our daughters, Kimberly and Kristina, have loved the Lord since they were little girls. They both married wonderful young men, Tim and Tom, who also love the Lord. Our oldest grandson, Cody, loves the Lord, and he married a beautiful young girl, Sierra, who loves the Lord. Our teenage granddaughter and grandson, Kaylee and Christopher, both accepted the Lord on the same day when they were only four years old. Corey and Chloe are the youngest of our grandsugars and they are being raised in the church and taught to love the Lord, also. I honestly cannot think of a greater blessing than this!

The next few pages are devotions that were written by our daughters. We added them to this book to demonstrate that, as the love of God is passed from one generation to the next generation, something wonderful and amazing happens. That way the torch is continually being passed from one generation to the next, so that the fire of God is never allowed to go out. That is the sacred responsibility of every Christian parent!

We have seen the power of this principle in action in a very poignant way recently in our own family. Our beautiful granddaughter, Kaylee, who recently turned 16 in January, was diagnosed with colon cancer when she was only 14. You will find that story in one of Kristina's devotions.

We have watched an amazing transformation happen in Kaylee since this trial began. We have watched her mature exponentially, even though the doctors said she would regress. It has been like watching a beautiful rosebud opening up and blossoming into an exquisitely gorgeous rose right before our eyes.

I attribute this phenomenon to two factors. One is the indomitable spirit of our granddaughter. She is determined and unstoppable! She reads her Bible voraciously, color codes it and writes notes all over the margins, then she draws doodles depicting the story about which she is reading. She has learned the value of continually filling herself with God's Word.

The doctors are amazed at her ability to continually bounce back. Her quick wit and sense of humor help keep everyone in good spirits. One day they were on a zoom call with the doctor, and he asked if he could talk to her. She does not like to talk about such unpleasant matters and feels like it weakens her faith, so when they asked if she would join them on the zoom call, she calmly replied, "I can't. Umm … I have to clean the gutters.". We were all in hysterics!

The other factor, however, which is the primary reason for Kaylee's strong foundation, is how her parents, Tim and Kristina, have been pouring the love and faith of God into her life since she was born. From the beginning, they have diligently taught her the Bible stories, faithfully made sure she was always in church, and showed her how to stand in faith and believe God for miracles. They didn't just *tell* her what to do, they *lived it*. She is now putting to use all the truths she has been taught all her life, and it has given her the strength and stamina needed to fight this very long battle. Their story is a perfect illustration of how God intended one generation to pass their faith on to the next generation.

May I earnestly encourage every parent reading this book to purpose in your heart to increase your efforts to pour the love of God into your children. We are living in difficult times and more than ever your children need to learn how to stand in faith. God handpicked us all to be alive on the earth at this time, and we need to make sure that not only are we walking in faith, but our children are, as well. There is a song by Dunsin Oyekan that says, *"An army is rising"*. We are that army -- all those who call themselves '*believers*'. May we use the days ahead to prepare ourselves and our families for whatever lies ahead, and keep looking up -- Jesus is coming!!

PRAYER – Dear Heavenly Father, I pray today that you will open my eyes to every opportunity I have to share God's love with my children. Show me creative ways to demonstrate how good and kind and faithful our God is, and that he can always be trusted to help us if we just call on him. Give me a sense of urgency so I will not waste valuable opportunities to impact their lives in a godly way. Thank you for helping me! AMEN

Do You Trust Me?

By Kimberly Ingram Murphy

Trust in the Lord with all your heart and lean
not on your own understanding. In all your
ways submit to him and he will make your
paths straight. Proverbs 3: 5-6 (NIV)

"Do you trust me?"

That is what my father asked me after he told me that he
felt strongly I was not supposed to go to the Youth Rally
we were scheduled to attend that night. We were getting
ready to leave and had over twenty young people going. We
had the exact number of cars we needed to accommodate
the group, and I strongly felt I should attend since I was the
Youth Leader.

"Why? What's wrong? Do I need to cancel the event?" I
asked.

"No, I feel it is *you* who are at risk", he replied, "and I am
asking *only you* to trust me and not go tonight".

Well, I had very conflicting thoughts on the matter. I
certainly didn't want to put myself at risk, and yet the whole
thing made no sense to me. What about the Youth Group?

They needed my car to carry some of the youth. I prayed for the strength and peace to change my plans. I chose to trust my father.

After calling the youth staff and reorganizing the plan for the night, I asked one of our big football players to drive my car to the rally. After they left for the rally, I felt such an urgency to pray for them, but at the same time, I had a deep peace knowing that I was exactly where I was supposed to be – at home!

It was on their way back from the Youth Rally that it happened. A drunk driver crossed over the double yellow lines and slammed into my car on the driver's side, exactly where I would have been sitting! The youth worker driving my car, along with all the passengers, were taken to the hospital for observation, and amazingly, not one of them was injured, other than a couple of bruises. The doctor spoke to the football player and said, "It's a good thing you are a big guy because that was a big crash! A smaller person would have been seriously injured, or even killed!"

My father had been led by the Lord! Had I not trusted him, I might not be alive today to write this testimony! Sometimes trust is VERY HARD, especially when it makes no sense. But trust anyway! God is trustworthy and promises to surely direct your path!

PRAYER – Lord, please help me today to be sensitive to that 'still, small voice' inside me, leading and directing me. Help me understand your instructions clearly and unmistakably and give me the grace to always be obedient – even when I don't understand. AMEN

Refuge & Shelter

By Kimberly Ingram Murphy

He will cover you with His feathers, and
under his wings you will find refuge.
Psalm 94:4 (NIV)

Most everyone remembers where they were on the day of 9/11. Whether you were directly or indirectly affected by the attack, the impact was felt by every American in deep and lasting ways. I drove home on my lunch hour that day to let my dog out and have a quick salad before returning to work. I turned on the news and there was the anchor in tears as she showed the video of the twin towers billowing with smoke.

As I listened to the report, I ran to call my husband. He had not heard the news report and was working in a town that had a large chemical plant and there had been some talk about safety issues. He was safe, but said he would button things up on the site.

I then called my parents who were on the road to North Carolina to visit my sister and her family who had been transferred there for her husband's work. Just days earlier my father had announced that they were *NOT* going to fly but would drive instead.

For some unknown reason he felt strongly that they were not to fly. A sixteen-hour drive versus a three-hour flight did not make sense, but they both knew to 'follow God's peace'. As it turned out, they would have been flying out of Logan Airport at the very time all the madness began. We were in awe at the safety and guidance God had provided them.

Later, my friends from New York City called. Their elementary-age niece whom they were raising was supposed to have been home hours ago and they could not reach anyone at the school. They were looking out their window and all they could see was smoke and soot covering all the buildings around them, and people were crying and yelling loudly on the streets. My friends began praying and calling on the name of Jesus!

We prayed with them and agreed together that their niece would make it home safely and they would be reunited shortly. It was less than an hour later when they called back. Their niece had made it home! She was covered in ashes and was physically and emotionally exhausted, but *SHE WAS HOME!* We were shouting praises over the phone!

The Lord never promised he would keep us *FROM* every trial and hardship, but that He would be *WITH* us through them. He said, "In this world you *WILL HAVE TRIBULATION* (trouble) but be of good cheer for I have overcome the world." John 16:33 (KJV)

He doesn't just *PROVIDE* refuge; He *IS* our refuge! The very word 'refuge' indicates that there is a 'storm' of some sort blowing from which you need to take shelter.

I love how the Lord gives words of truth all through the Scriptures that apply to everyday situations. He knew that life would sometimes bring wind and rain and He comforts us by reminding us that we can *COME UNDER HIS WINGS AND WAIT OUT THE STORM!*

Whether your 'storm' is large or small, God's wings are big enough to provide all the shelter you need. His refuge not only shields us but offers guidance and insight into the situation so you can walk safely in the steps he has specifically designed for you to walk. "The steps of a righteous man are ordered by the Lord, and he delights in his way. Though he stumbles, he will not fall for the Lord upholds him with his hand." Psalm 37:23-24 (KJV)

MAKE THE LORD YOUR REFUGE! RUN TO HIM FOR SHELTER! LET HIM DIRECT YOUR STEPS! THERE IS NO SAFER PLACE THAN SAFETY IN THE ARMS OF JESUS!

PRAYER – Lord, I thank you for your Word that promises to help us in our time of need. I pray for your help and protection today, whether we are at work, at school, at home, or in the car. Wherever we may be, keep your everlasting arms around us and guide us in paths of safety, and we will give you praise and honor! AMEN

Stand Alone Noah Faith

By Kimberly Ingram Murphy

Noah was a righteous man, blameless among
the people of his time, and he walked
faithfully with God. Genesis 6:9 (NIV)

I have always been intrigued by the story of Noah and the Ark. It amazes me that he had the faith to build a structure that took him 120 years to complete without the support of anyone in his community, nor the rest of the entire population of the earth! Noah stood alone in his faith in God his Creator! He was not swayed by the jeers of the crowd as they mocked him for building a giant ark in the middle of the desert. He did not succumb to the voices of society in that day.

Can't you just hear the crowd taunting him?! "Noah, think of your poor children! The humiliation is too much! If God REALLY told you to build a boat, wouldn't He have helped you complete it sooner? We have never seen rain, and yet you are building a giant sailing vessel! Give up this foolish dream of yours!"

But Noah did not listen to the crowd. Noah kept his eyes on the project and had such communion with his heavenly Father, it gave him courage to finish the divine task he had been given. When your teenager is discouraged and feels that he is the only Christian in his school, remind him of Noah. Noah was the only righteous man *ON THE ENTIRE EARTH!*

If Noah could stay strong in his faith and trust in the Lord all alone ... SO CAN WE!

When I was six years old, the Lord called my father to leave Texas and move to New England to pioneer a church. Many people tried to talk him out of it, including his relatives. They told him he was being selfish taking his children away from their grandparents and cousins. Knowing how much my father loves his family, I know it was hard for him to hear those words. He knew, however, what the Lord had told him, and he refused to be distracted or discouraged by the voices of the crowd.

We sold everything we owned and moved to Rhode Island. We started a church there and saw hundreds of souls come to the saving knowledge of Jesus. Those beautiful people are still serving the Lord today and have led countless others to Christ. We cannot let the crowd dictate what decisions we make or how we will live out our faith.

BE BOLD! BE STRONG! FOR THE LORD OUR GOD IS WITH US ALWAYS!

PRAYER –Lord, please help me to have the courage to obey your voice even if no one else is standing with me. Help me to walk out my faith boldly and affect my generation. Let me be reminded of Noah, Ruth, Esther and many others who had the faith to stand alone and go against the 'norm' of their day. Let me be mighty in you and see your hand accomplish what only you can do. Let me be your vessel through which you can 'build an ark'. Let me never be afraid to stand, even if it is against a crowd. Thank you that you promised to never leave me nor forsake me. You are faithful and I trust you! AMEN

We Are Many Parts, But One Body

By Kimberly Ingram Murphy

Even so the body is not made up of one part
but of many. I Corinthians 12:14 (NIV)

God created the body so unique, so special and multi-faceted. It is amazing how even the smallest, seemingly insignificant part of our body is vital. We often do not realize it until it is not working right, or actually gets broken. Each part is a piece of the puzzle and proves just how true the scripture is that says, "I am fearfully and wonderfully made." Psalm 139:14 (NIV)

Shortly after school started one year, my second-grader twisted her wrist jumping off the monkey bars toward the end of recess. Although she was not in a lot of pain, it was obvious something wasn't right. X-rays revealed she had a "subtle buckle of the distal radius". After asking the doctor if that was actually a 'real thing', he grinned and said, "Yes, it's real. It's a very tiny fracture and if we don't set it in a cast, it could deter her later in her gymnastics and other athletics".

During her time in a cast she had to alter how she did everything. She was not allowed to play at recess or in gym class, she needed help to open water bottles, she had to wear a special plastic bag over the cast to take a bath, and she had to keep her arm propped on a pillow to sleep comfortably. It was a break so tiny that they call it a 'subtle buckle', and yet it played a huge role in how she lived each day. We quickly learned that a Distal Radius is a very important little bone.

I could not help but think of the scripture in 1 Corinthians 12 that explains how we are many parts, but one body. That little 'distal radius' was *VERY NECESSARY* and affected how she was able, or unable, to live and move. It is much the same in the Body of Christ. *WE NEED EACH OTHER!* We all have a role to play and when we are not 'rightly joined together', the entire body suffers!

The enemy of our soul wants us to feel like we are insignificant and not necessary, but nothing could be further from the truth! Each of us plays an important role in the Body of Christ. He gave each of us different gifts, talents and abilities with which to serve the Lord, the church, and one another. There is *NO ONE* who is insignificant! Everyone is needed!

1 Corinthians 12:16-20 (NIV) says, "And if the ear should say, 'because I am not an eye, I do not belong to the body', it would not for that reason stop being a part of the body. If the whole body were an eye, where would the sense of hearing be? If the whole body were an ear where would the sense of smell be? But in fact, God has placed the parts of the body, every one of them, just as he wanted them to be. If there were only one part, where would the body be? As it is, there are many parts, but one body."

You may have a different ability than your brother or sister in Christ, but all are necessary and vital. Be determined to be who God made *YOU* and use what he has put inside you to complete the body. If you are a 'distal radius' in the wrist, do not try to be the 'hamstring' in the leg. Your particular role makes the body work properly. So, thank the Lord for who you are, and use your 'part' to bless others and further the Kingdom of God.

PRAYER – Lord, I thank you for creating me with my particular personality, abilities and talents to fulfill my divine destiny. Help me to see myself through *YOUR* eyes, so I can stand against the lies of the enemy. I thank you that I have an important part in your Kingdom, and I *WILL* do my best to fulfill what you purpose for me. I will love the rest of the body of Christ and do all I can to stay strong in you so I can keep my 'part' healthy. Thank you for loving me enough to create me! AMEN

Nothing To Fear

By Kimberly Ingram Murphy

Precious in the sight of the Lord is the death
of his faithful servants. Psalm 116:15 (NIV)

I have sat at the hospital bedside of dying saints with my dad
through the years. I have read the Psalms to them and sang
the hymns of our faith. I have watched their fragile smiles
as they join with me in singing.

In particular, one woman I remember had only a few days
to live, and all of her children were called to fly home. She
asked me to come and sing to her and her children, several
of whom were unsaved. She had a song list of her favorite
songs ready for me, and her frail voice gathered strength as
she joined in the singing, taking her children's hands and
singing to them directly. Everyone had tears flowing down
their faces.

As she sang to them, she said, "I'm not afraid! I'll be singing
in the heavenly choir soon. Jesus loves me and he loves
you, too!" She then took my hand and held it to her face
and told me to never stop singing for Jesus. Her peace was
undeniable! Jesus' perfect love had cast out her fear because
she had allowed his love to fill her heart.

Satan will do all he can to inflict fear on us and try to rob us of peace. Financial trouble, family crisis, sickness, and workplace woes are just a scratch on the surface of the tactics he uses to inflict fear into our lives. When fear tries to grip us, we need only to remember his promise that he will never leave us or forsake us. "What time I am afraid, I will trust in you, Lord." Psalm 56:3 (KJV) We, as the children of God, have the peace of knowing that the Lord walks with us even in the darkest moments of our lives. Psalm 23 reminds us that even when we walk through the valley of the shadow of death, we will fear no evil for *GOD IS WITH US!*

If we don't fear death, is there really anything to fear?

PRAYER – Lord, I thank you for all the promises you gave us in your Word, that you would care for us, guide and direct us, provide for us, and most of all that you would never leave us. Even in death you will be with us, giving us strength and courage. You are a loving Heavenly Father, and we trust you with every area of our lives! AMEN

I Know My Father's Voice

By Kristina Ingram Chambers

"My sheep hear My voice, and I know them,
and they follow Me." John 10:27 (KJV)

Many years ago, while on a family vacation in San Marcus, Texas, we went for a hike in the woods. I was walking ahead of my family on the trail, unaware of any dangers that may befall us. As I was walking, I heard my Dad's voice yell, "JUMP"!!! I didn't turn around and ask … was that my Father's voice; are you talking to me; why do you want me to jump? I didn't ask questions, I just jumped.

As he continued yelling, "JUMP, AND DON"T STOP!" I realized why I was jumping. A very large, colorful snake had wrapped itself around my leg. As I jumped, it loosened the snake's hold and it fell onto my feet and slithered off into the woods, thankfully without biting me.

That incident made me think of how we should listen to our Heavenly Father's voice. For some reason we tend to question when we hear his voice. We question it for several reasons such as … was that really God's voice? Or maybe it is not something we really want to do. So many times, though, listening to that voice could spare us from trouble or even possibly save our lives as listening to my father's voice in the woods did that day.

How do we hear God's voice? Craig von Buseck on CBN said, "God wants to fellowship and communicate with us. That's two-way communication. Why? Because you can't really have a relationship unless there is true dialogue. How do we get to know a person? By communicating with them. By talking and listening. It's the same with our relationship with God. He talks, we listen. We talk, he listens."

As we build that relationship with God and communicate with him on a daily basis, we learn to hear his voice and what it sounds like, just like we know what our earthly father's voice sounds like. The Bible even says we can hear God's voice in John 10:27 (KJV), "My sheep hear my voice, and I know them, and they follow me." Also, in Isaiah 30:21 (NIV), "Your ears shall hear a word behind you, saying, this is the way, walk in it,"

So take time each day to communicate with God, not only talking to him, but be sure to stop and listen, so you can hear his voice!

That day I jumped, I didn't ask questions because I knew my father's voice … do you know your father's voice?

PRAYER – Lord, thank you that you love us enough to speak to us, and thank you that you gave us the ability to hear your voice. Help me to keep my ears and my heart open to hear when you speak. Let me be like Samuel when the Lord called him and he simply said, "Here am I". AMEN

He Knows My Name

By Kristina Ingram Chambers

"...yet you know me, Lord; you see me."
Jeremiah 12:3 (NIV)

Do you ever feel invisible? Do you feel like no one notices you or knows your name? Take heart because God knows your name.

I love the song by Francesca Battistelli called, "He Knows My Name". The words say, "I don't need my name in lights, I'm famous in my Father's eyes, make no mistake, He knows my name. I'm not living for applause, I'm already so adored, it's all His stage, He knows my name."

There is a running joke among our family and friends that I am the Invisible Person. I could tell story after story where I have been forgotten or invisible to others. I have even spent half my life answering to names other than my own, many times by people who have known me for many, many years. The most common names people call me are Kim, Samantha and Sue ... nothing close to my own name, Kristina. LOL. But I answer to them, so I won't embarrass people.

The funniest story to me was the most recent where I went to a conference and saw an acquaintance that I have had contact with over the past 11 years. This person introduced themselves to me every day of the three-day conference, saying it was nice to meet me each day. LOL .

I have learned through the years that it doesn't matter if no one remembers me or knows my name because GOD DOES! So, I just laugh about it and find it rather funny.

Don't go through life worrying about being noticed or if people know your name. God knows your name and sees everything you do and you are famous in your Father's eyes! Don't live for others to notice you ... everything you do, do as unto the Lord!

When no one knows the hours you prayed on your knees for them ... God does!

When no one sees all the behind-the-scenes work you've done ... God does!

When no one sees you or notices you ... God does!

When no one knows your name ... God does!

PRAYER – Thank you that when you hung on that cross, my name was on your mind. Thank you for being such a loving, caring, wonderful heavenly Father to your children. Thank you that you know my name! AMEN

Choose Joy

By Kristina Ingram Chambers

Consider it pure joy, my brothers & sisters,
whenever you face trials of many kinds.
James 1:2 (NIV)

Be joyful in hope, patient in affliction, and
faithful in prayer. Romans 12:12 (NIV)

These things have I spoken unto you, that
my joy might remain in you, & that your joy
might be full. John 15:11 (KJV)

Be joyful in hope. Romans 12:12 (NIV)

2020 was a tough year for our family. Well, it was obviously a tough year for everyone. The first few weeks of the lockdown, however, were kind of fun—we played endless hours of games, watched countless movies, worked on puzzles, etc ... it was almost like a staycation. Then the weeks turned into months and no one was having fun anymore. We all missed seeing our family and friends and everyone started to feel isolated. We didn't think 2020 could get any worse, and then it did ...

In May of 2020 our 14 year old daughter was diagnosed with colon cancer, extremely rare in adolescence. Nothing can ever prepare you to hear a diagnosis like this for your child! 2020 continued to get even worse ...

Only one parent was allowed in the hospital at this time, so I was alone with our daughter, trying to keep my emotions in check. We were not allowed to leave the room due to the lockdown, so I had to try to keep the tears at bay in front of my daughter. It was 2:00 am in the morning that first night and I sat on the side of my bed weeping when a nurse came in with all her alien-looking hazmat garb. She sat on the side of the bed next to me and just put her arm around me and sat with me.

The next morning another nurse came in and said, "You must know someone high up because they are going to let your husband come in". We knew no one high up at the hospital. Actually, we didn't know anyone at the hospital, but we knew Someone higher up than that. We knew God had intervened on our behalf.

Those first few days we thought we would never stop crying and never smile again. We were told by the doctors that this journey would be a marathon, not a sprint. Our daughter, of course, had many times of tears, but when meeting with doctor after doctor, she would dry the tears, sit and listen, and ask the most adult-like questions. We were told by a specialist that when children have a diagnosis like this, they tend to regress at least by a year. We didn't see that, and instead saw her grow up overnight and handle it better than most adults.

It has been a year and a half now and we are still running the marathon and she is still in treatment. She has had major surgery, many procedures, immunotherapy, chemo, radiation, and through it all, we have seen our daughter's faith grow and doctors be amazed at how well she feels. Our family motto has become, *"CHOOSE JOY!"* Sometimes we have to remind each other of that, but it has helped us through so many situations. The doctors say they know her outlook has helped her!

Through it all, she rarely ever misses youth group or church or anything else she wants to do. There are times when we say, "Why don't you stay home and rest". She always says, "Why? ... I'm fine!" She has several t-shirts that she wears to treatment that say, "It's fine, I'm fine, everything's fine!"

We have many people say to us, "You shouldn't be smiling ... why are you smiling ... how are you smiling?" Of course, we are not smiling because of what we are going through, but you see, we have truly learned that the joy of the Lord is not just for when things are going good. When you put your trust and faith in Him, it's like Nehemiah 8:10 (KJV) says, " ...the joy of the Lord is my strength."

If you are going through difficult times, put your trust and faith in God and pray for the joy of the Lord to be your strength. CHOOSE JOY!

PRAYER – Thank you for your loving care no matter what we are going through. Please give me the grace to always remember your faithfulness even in the difficult times. Help me to always CHOOSE JOY! AMEN

CPSIA information can be obtained
at www.ICGtesting.com
Printed in the USA
BVHW042119130722
641717BV00002B/10